BLACK HILLS
CAMPING

YOUR GUIDE TO PUBLIC CAMPGROUNDS IN
WESTERN SOUTH DAKOTA AND NORTHEASTERN WYOMING

MARC SMITH

Open Space
Publications
Casper, Wyoming

Direct all inquiries to:
Open Space Publications, LLC
PO Box 50133
Casper, WY 82605-0133

Visit our website: www.OpenSpacePublications.com

ISBN 978-0-9740900-6-1
Library of Congress Control Number: 2011928635

Proudly printed in the United States of America
First Edition

Photos by author unless otherwise credited.
Edited by Judith Savala-Wright.
Cover design by Julie Cornia of Black Dog Design.

Caution

Camping and outdoor recreation are potentially dangerous activities that pose risks. The author and publisher assume no responsibility or liability for any damages, losses, accidents, or injuries incurred from using this book. It is the reader's responsibility to be aware of all risks and take the necessary precautions to handle those risks.

While the author has made considerable attempts to make this book as accurate as possible, errors may exist. Campground facilities, management, roads, and usage can and do change. All maps and distances are for general reference only and should be supplemented with maps produced by the managing agencies.

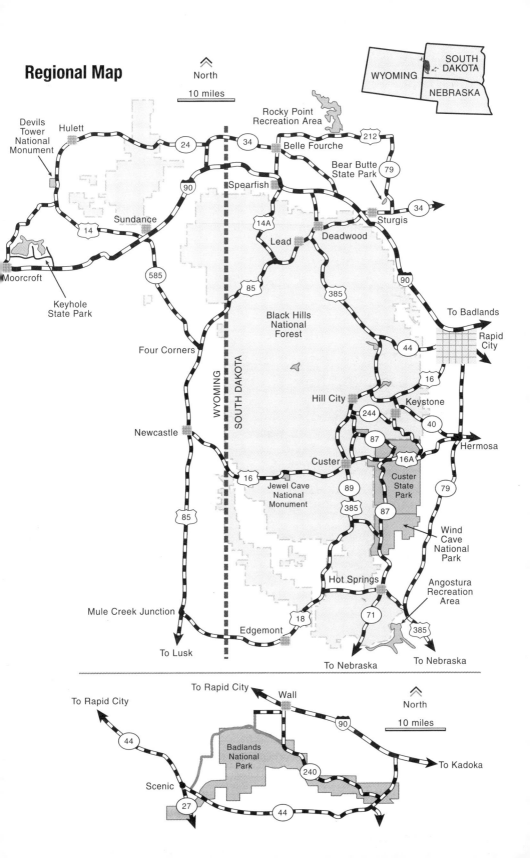

Road Abbreviations

FR	Forest Road; these roads are located within the Black Hills National Forest and managed by the USDA Forest Service.
CR	County Road; these roads are managed by the county. Road numbers often change when you cross a county line.
HWY	Highway (both Federal and State); state highway numbers change when you cross a state line.
I	Interstate Highway.

Map Legend

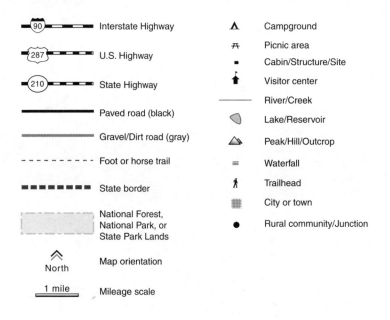

90	Interstate Highway
287	U.S. Highway
210	State Highway
	Paved road (black)
	Gravel/Dirt road (gray)
	Foot or horse trail
	State border
	National Forest, National Park, or State Park Lands
North	Map orientation
1 mile	Mileage scale

▲	Campground
⊼	Picnic area
▪	Cabin/Structure/Site
♦	Visitor center
—	River/Creek
◐	Lake/Reservoir
△	Peak/Hill/Outcrop
=	Waterfall
⚐	Trailhead
▦	City or town
●	Rural community/Junction

Contents

Southern Black Hills 79

Preface

I visited the Black Hills of Wyoming at least a half dozen times to research the area for my other guidebooks. I had also taken a few touristy trips into western South Dakota. So when I decided to write a camping book that included all of the Black Hills, I suspected that I'd have to make at least one more trip to the Hills, maybe two. Was I ever wrong. Only after I had spent a week camping in South Dakota did I realize how many things there are to see and do. A lot of information on the Black Hills can be found on the web, but it's surprisingly incomplete and inaccurate. I quickly realized that this was going to be a lot more work than expected (and it always is).

Over the next few years, I returned to the area another five times to camp, hike, visit attractions, ask questions, and just get to know this fascinating region. Even as this book was being readied for print in 2011, I found myself driving 1,100 miles in two days to get a few more photos and verify a list of tidbits. I've learned that you never stop exploring and that research for a book like this never really ends—there is always something that can be added. When I return to the Hills in the future, I'll discover even more treasures. You surely will too.

Acknowledgements

My first acknowledgement goes to my wife and two daughters. It's not always easy to pack up the camper and leave home (especially with infants), but we've done that time and again. Julie, thanks for having an adventurous spirit and tolerating many long days of driving. Some of those miles were rough (baby screaming, vehicle overheating on a hot summer day), and I appreciate you pushing through. I also need to thank my parents, Jo Ann and Merrill Smith, and my nephew Brent Fuchs for the time they joined us and gave us their support. William Cownover, my brother-in-law, dropped everything at a moment's notice to go on a lightning quick trip with me through the Hills.

There are a few more individuals to mention. Mike Hambleton joined me for an awesome trip that took us from the Red Desert of southwestern Wyoming to the tops of the Black Hills. George Janson and Brian and Katy Walsh gave me scores of photos, some of which you'll find in this book. Julie Cornia once again provided her outstanding creative design. Judith Wright squeezed in another editing project with little notice. Thank you, each one of you.

As a whole, I'd like to mention the government agencies in and around the Black Hills, particularly the Forest Service. Over the years, I've worked with many different national forests. None of them have been as knowledgeable and helpful as those individuals on the Black Hills National Forest. The US Corps of Engineers also went out of their way to answer my questions.

INTRODUCTION
WHAT TO KNOW BEFORE YOU GO

Amidst the Great Plains, near the geographical doorstep of the Rocky Mountains, you'll find an isolated, mountainous island. Known to the Lakota Indians as Paha Sapa—hills that are black—the dark timbered highland, and the country surrounding it, is full of intrigue and wonder.

Set atop the geological center of the non-contiguous United States, the Black Hills region is America's playground. Boasting an impressive concentration of national parks, national monuments, national forests, state parks, museums, amusement parks, wildlife exhibits, and organized rallies, the region has something for everyone. Millions come here annually to visit these attractions and many take advantage of the area's outdoor grandeur by making their trip a camping vacation.

This guide sorts out the dozens of campgrounds available to you. You'll find where to stay, what you need to know about your camp, and what to do once you get there. Let's get started!

History

When dinosaurs roamed the earth, they must have been fond of Black Hills country. The area is well known for being fossil rich, and many meaningful ones have been excavated. Perhaps the most famous is Sue, the largest Tyrannosaurus rex ever found that is now on display at The Field Museum in Chicago.

Fast forwarding to the 19th century, the area's dominant American Indian tribe was the Lakota, also called the Sioux. Gold was suspected in the Black Hills and in 1874, Lt. Colonel George Custer led an expedition to the Hills to investigate. The presence of gold was confirmed, and the rush was on—the settlement of the area began just a year later. Indian treaties soon followed, and it wasn't long before the natives were pushed off their prized lands and onto reservations.

The first railroad was built in 1881, and others soon followed. With railroad tracks came the demand for railroad ties. Thus, the Black Hills' timber industry was born (and continues to be a productive industry today). By 1897, much of the area's timbered portion was designated as the Black Hills Forest Reserve. A decade later, the reserve became the Black Hills National Forest after the creation of the USDA Forest Service.

Tourism began around the turn of the 20th century and never stopped. Today, the area is dotted with souvenir shops, tourist traps (some tacky, some worthwhile), visitor centers, amusement parks, and exhibits. The area's popularity has also attracted organized rallies, such as the Sturgis Motorcycle Rally that is attended by hundreds of thousands of bikers each year.

Today, the area is home to roughly 200,000 residents, including some 70,000 who live in Rapid City, the region's largest city. Part of this population lives in the mountains themselves, and you'll find that there are considerable private holdings within the national forest.

If the history of the Black Hills is of interest to you, you'll find a plethora of books that cover topics such as the railroads, gold rush, Civilian Conservation Corps, outlaws, and the displacement of the American Indians. Once you're in the area, you'll enjoy a fine selection of museums, visitor centers, and historical sites.

The Land

Much of western South Dakota and eastern Wyoming are covered by vast grasslands, some publicly owned. Contrasting with these flatlands, the rugged Black Hills are impossible to miss. Stretching roughly 120 miles north-south and 65 miles east-west, the mountains have a complex and diverse geology.

On the outskirts, the Hills are flanked by geological wonders and natural treasures. To the west, Devils Tower—a huge column of rock—pierces the bright sky. Flanking the tower is the Thunder Basin National

Grassland, which holds this nation's largest open coal mines. South and east of the Black Hills is the Buffalo Gap National Grassland with more sprawling prairies of mixed grass. Also east of the Hills are badlands that form colorful pinnacles and bluffs that are replete with fossils.

The Hills themselves are surrounded by an outer ring of sandstone that creates hogbacks and ponderosa pine-speckled rims that rise hundreds of feet above the plains. Inside this ring is a second geological feature of red sandstone known as the Red Valley or Race Track.

Limestone is among the various rocks that comprise the higher Hills and it forms a plateau that covers hundreds, if not thousands, of miles of caves and caverns. Some of these can be explored, such as those found at Wind Cave National Park and Jewel Cave National Monument.

The inner, highest core of the Hills is granite, which forms a beautiful compilation of outcrops, peaks, and unique spires known as the Needles. This core—covering around a quarter of the total area of the Black Hills— culminates to Harney Peak (7,242 feet), South Dakota's highest point and the tallest mountain east of the Rocky Mountains. In all, there are 18 peaks here that exceed 7,000 feet.

Although each of these geological structures is distinct, most visitors find that they blend together without much notice. The fine mix of forests, canyons, meadows, peaks, and grasslands create a singular splendor that will have you reaching for your camera time and again.

Weather and Climate

By Rocky Mountain standards, the Black Hills have a moderate climate that is well suited for camping. That's not to say that turbulent weather doesn't happen. The type of weather you encounter depends largely on where and when you visit.

The northern Black Hills around Deadwood receive about 30 inches of annual precipitation. Only half of that is received in the southern Hills. These southern reaches are also warmer. In fact, Hot Springs is considered one of the warmest locales in South Dakota.

The traditional camping season begins with the two wettest months, May and June. Muddy conditions and some cool, soupy days can be expected during this period. By July, drier and warmer weather patterns emerge. The higher mountainous terrain of the Black Hills offers some relief from summertime heat. Common daytime highs are in the 70s and 80s, though heat waves can usher in temperatures in the 90s. Evenings and nights are very comfortable. With nighttime lows in the 50s, you can usually get by with a light sleeping bag or blanket.

Unfortunately, brilliant summer mornings often give way to thunderstorms in the afternoons and evenings. Though many of these will result in nothing but a few rumbles and afternoon sprinkles, some will become severe. Be aware of hazards such as lightning, flash flooding, gusty winds, hail, and even microbursts—damaging tornado-like downdrafts.

The tail end of summer and autumn are excellent times to visit the region. Mild temperatures, fewer storms and crowds, and changing fall colors are all reasons to consider visiting in late August, September, and October.

Though winter brings snow and cold temperatures, many campgrounds remain open in some capacity during these months. If you're willing to brave bone-chilling winds and temperatures that can range anywhere from the single digits to the 40s, you'll easily find a campsite. A few good snowstorms can be expected each winter and a significant blizzard slams the area every few years.

Flora

The plants and trees growing in and around the Black Hills vary greatly depending on terrain, elevation, and geography. The landscape can change dramatically over a relatively small distance, offering you ever-changing scenery as you explore the area.

The flats and rolling prairies below the Black Hills are comprised of mixed grasses and plants such as sagebrush, yucca, and prickly pear cactus. In drier and rockier terrain, you'll find Rocky Mountain juniper and shrubs like mountain mahogany.

Higher elevations mean more trees. Although the northern and western areas of the Black Hills have substantial stands of white spruce, the lion's share of the forest is comprised of ponderosa pine, a distinctive evergreen with long needles and thick, orange-red bark. These pine forests are managed very actively and you'll find many acres of thinned forests, which have a clean, manicured appearance. Conversely, forest fires have transformed some swaths of forest into charred, open woodland. You'll also find trees that have turned red or no longer have needles. These are dead pines that likely have been attacked by the mountain pine beetle, a destructive pest that has created a widespread epidemic across the West. Use extreme caution when recreating in pine-killed forests. Trees falling and killing people have already made headlines.

The Black Hills hold a greater variety of deciduous trees than mountainous areas further west, especially along wetter areas such as stream banks. Bur oak, willow, cottonwood, and quaking aspen are a few that you'll find. To find these trees during the peak color season, visit the Hills in early to mid-October.

Other plants to note include wildflowers and there are many of them. Rocky Mountain iris, Indian paintbrush, bluebell, and black-eyed Susan are just a few that can be found. Peak seasons and locations vary by species, but you can usually find color throughout late spring and summer.

Poison ivy is one plant in the Black Hills that you'll hope to not find. The old saying, "Leaves of three, leave it be" is only helpful if you can differentiate poison ivy from a slew of other plants that only have three

Western Poison Ivy –George Janson photo

leaves. Instead, take note of the leaves themselves, which vary greatly in size. Look for pointed leaves that have irregular edges (they can be jagged or smooth). The middle leaf has a longer stalk, while the other two leaves connect closely to the stem. The top of the leaves appears waxy or glossy and has a different color depending on the season.

To avoid the misery associated with poison ivy—severe itching, blisters, rash—wear long pants and watch where you walk and what you touch. Poison ivy is most prevalent in thick vegetation along stream banks and draws and is less common at higher elevations.

Wildlife

Wild animals thrive in the Black Hills and adjacent lands. The diversity that this region offers—from low grasslands to towering granite spires— invites a mix of species that you normally wouldn't see in the same area (like mountain goats and rattlesnakes).

Among the most common animals you'll spot, particularly in Custer State Park and Badlands National Park, are buffalo (properly known as American Bison). You'll find them on roads and parking lots and in grassland prairies and small clearings. Weighing up to a hefty 2,000 pounds, bison can appear docile and sluggish. Don't be fooled. These animals are quite dangerous and can run more than 35 mph, so keep a safe distance.

Other common ungulates that reside in the region include elk, mule deer, and whitetail deer. Pronghorn antelope are also present, as are Rocky Mountain Bighorn sheep. You may even spy white mountain goats around

Keep watch for bison along roads, trails, and in camp –Katy Walsh photo

the granite outcroppings in the southern Black Hills. There have been a pair of moose spottings in recent years, but these were believed to be transient animals.

On the Wildlife Loop Road in Custer State Park, you'll likely encounter a few feral burros standing along the road looking for a food handout, though park staff discourages feeding them. These are the descendants of donkeys that were originally brought here in the 1920s to be used as pack animals.

To many tent campers' relief, there are no grizzly bears in the Black Hills. There are generally no black bears either. However, a few black bears have been sighted in Wyoming's side of the Hills and in the grasslands to the southwest, so there is a possibility that the area could regain a sustainable population of these bruins in the future.

Other predators that you're not likely to encounter, though they do live in the Hills, are in the cat family. Mountain lions—also known as cougars—have made a comeback in this region and are increasing in other Midwestern states as well. Other cats that secretly live here include the bobcat and perhaps a small number of lynx. While researching this book, I was fortunate enough to catch glimpses of two of these cats—a mountain lion with a tracking collar outside of Hot Springs and a small but stout bobcat on a remote gravel road near Dalton Lake.

Although these nocturnal creatures are typically very shy around humans and sleep throughout much of the day, they still pose a risk, especially to children. In the unlikely event that you encounter a mountain lion, it is important that you do not act like prey. Increase your height by standing on a log or rock to appear more intimidating. If you have a child, pick him or her up. If you have a jacket on, you can fan the sides out to look wider. Wave, throw stones, and make noise. The effort will usually send the lion running away. If you are attacked, fight back using anything and everything that you have. People have survived mountain lion attacks by fighting back with their bare hands, by using rocks, or small pocketknives.

Smaller animals that you might hear or see include coyotes, fox, skunks, beavers, squirrels, raccoons, yellow-belly marmots, porcupines, and badgers. One tourist favorite is prairie dogs, which are seen scurrying around their colonies of holes and tunnels. These critters are an important food source for black-footed ferrets, which were once on the brink of extinction. Efforts are underway across the West to repopulate these elusive predators. In South Dakota, the ferrets have been reintroduced to a half dozen sites since the 1990s.

You'll find plenty of birds in the Black Hills. On the ground, watch for Merriam turkeys. A couple dozen of these game birds were introduced for hunting here a half century ago and they are now believed to number nearly 20,000. Among the birds that take flight, you may spot red-tailed hawks, falcons, golden eagles, northern goshawk, woodpeckers, and nearly 200 other species that live in or migrate through the area.

Rattlesnakes deserve special attention when recreating in Black Hills country. In South Dakota and eastern Wyoming, you'll find the prairie rattlesnake which can vary slightly in color. Some may be light brown, but the ones I've encountered in the Black Hills have had a greenish tint, making them difficult to see in thick understory and on shrubby trails.

When hiking, use a hiking pole and watch your footing. If you encounter a rattler, keep your distance and let it slither away. Remember that these snakes can strike at a distance of half their body length. In the unfortunate event that you suffer a bite, be assured that rattlers are rarely lethal. Forget all those snakebite remedies that involve ice, sucking devices, and tourniquets. Experts advise that you remain calm, remove clothing or items (such as rings) that may interfere with swelling, immobilize the bite area, and get to the hospital as soon as possible. If you can, draw a circle around the bite site and note the time—this will help medical providers determine the severity of the bite, which may or may not contain venom.

Prairie rattler –Katy Walsh photo

When considering things that bite, remember ticks and mosquitoes! Deer ticks can transmit very serious diseases to humans if they are attached to the skin for longer than a day or two. Mosquitoes can carry a disease called West Nile Virus. The best way to deter these pests is to use a repellent and wear long sleeves and pants. Check yourself periodically. If you find a tick that's lodged, pull it straight out with tweezers, getting as close to its head as possible, then wash and cover the area.

Viewing Wildlife

Here are a few tips for viewing wildlife:

- Get up early and stay out late. Animals are most active during the cooler parts of the day. This is usually from sunrise to 10:00 a.m. and from 4:00 p.m. till dark. Animals are also more active during cooler, cloudy days but less active during periods of rain or snow.

- When you are in likely habitat, use binoculars or a spotting scope to "glass" the area. In many cases, animals will be bedded down and may be hard to find. Look for dark spots or specific parts of an animal, such as antlers, just above the grass or brush.

- If you spot wildlife, stay quiet, avoid sudden movements, and try not to disturb the animals. Wildlife that feels threatened or bothered by your presence will quickly move out of the area. If you have a pet, keep it in the vehicle. A barking dog can be a great liability when you are near wild animals.

- Zoom in or use a telephoto lens to capture a closer picture instead of approaching an animal. Never honk, yell, or throw anything to get an animal's attention. This may actually motivate it to move farther away.

Camping Options

With several state parks, a national forest, two national parks, two national monuments, state-owned land, and dozens of privately-owned campgrounds, the Black Hills area has plenty of campsites. When looking for a place to camp, you have three primary choices that range from primitive to borderline luxurious.

Public Campgrounds

This book includes all of the developed public campgrounds in the Black Hills area. These camps are maintained by one of several government agencies including the National Park Service, USDA Forest Service, South Dakota Game, Fish and Parks, U.S. Army Corps of Engineers, and Wyoming Game & Fish. The majority of public campgrounds do not offer hookups or services like those found at a privately-owned campground, but several of the most popular camps in the Black Hills do. Most camps have potable water, pit toilets, picnic tables, fire rings, and trash containers. Many campgrounds have on-site hosts between Memorial Day and Labor Day to help maintain campground facilities and assist campers.

Public campgrounds require campers to follow a few reasonable campground rules and regulations. These rules include a designated quiet time (usually between 10:00 p.m. and 6:00 a.m.) and keeping your pets leashed or under control. In addition, riding ATVs on campground roads is not allowed unless you are entering or exiting a paid site. Each campground posts its own rules and regulations at the pay station or fee board.

Dispersed Camping

Dispersed camping is nothing more than finding an area you like on national forest land and setting up camp. By doing so, you'll carry the responsibility of properly handling your trash and human waste as well as preserving the general condition of the land.

Certain rules apply when dispersed camping. You must camp 50 feet from a road, stream, or trail. The length of stay is limited to 14 days within a 60-day period at the campsite and immediate vicinity. You can not disperse camp next to reservoirs or developed campgrounds. Also, dispersed campers can build campfires in Wyoming (depending on fire conditions), but not in South Dakota.

No charge or permit is required to disperse camp, but keep in mind that you cannot use the services or facilities of a nearby public campground without paying. If you choose to camp in this manner, please do so with a low-impact attitude and contact the Forest Service for current regulations.

Privately-owned Campgrounds

Privately-owned campgrounds, such as RV parks, are found in towns and along main highways. Although the most costly, these types of campgrounds are great for campers who want more facilities and services than public campgrounds offer. Most private camps offer water, electric, and sewer hookups as well as TV and Internet access. Other amenities can include a small store, showers, cabins, swimming pool, arcade, and miniature golf course.

Camping Suggestions

Here are a number of simple suggestions to make your camping trip more enjoyable.

- For those campgrounds that accept or require reservations, such as those in Custer State Park, get reservations as early as possible. Many campsites in Custer are reserved many months in advance. For campgrounds that operate on a first-come, first-served basis, plan on arriving by the early afternoon to secure a site. For popular camps, such as those near Mount Rushmore, arrive in the early morning if you don't have reservations—you may be able to score a recently vacated site. Many campgrounds fill by Friday afternoon on a busy holiday weekend.

- Take a grill or cooking stove in case there are fire restrictions in the area where you are camping. Campfires are sometimes prohibited in late summer or in drought years when dry conditions advance the fire danger.

- Bringing your own firewood to the Black Hills is discouraged. In fact, in Custer State Park out-of-state firewood is prohibited and you are asked to turn it over to the campground host if you have it. Fortunately, many campground hosts and stores offer firewood for sale by the bundle. If you're camping in the Black Hills National Forest, you won't have much luck scavenging for wood in campgrounds as they are already stripped clean of all deadfall. If your campground host doesn't sell firewood, you can collect some out in the forest. Only collect what you will use, though, as you'll need a forest product permit if you take it with you.

  On a related note, be responsible with your campfire and maintain a reasonable size. There is no need to outblaze your camp neighbors. It is becoming more common to pass on the firefighting costs to the person responsible (or irresponsible, rather).

Outdoor Ethics

Outdoor recreationists can leave the land as they found it and minimize the signs of use by embracing low-impact techniques. With increasing numbers of visitors on public lands, it is simply vital that we all do our part. Techniques to reduce the impact to our land vary slightly depending on their source, but the basic concepts are listed here.

- Find a campsite instead of making one. Camp on durable surfaces such as rock, gravel, dry grass, or snow. Leave rocks, plants, and other natural objects as you found them. Do not build structures or dig trenches around tents.

- In the backcountry, travel single file along designated trails. Travel in small groups of four to six people to reduce the impact on a given area. Yield to people you meet on the trail and step to the downhill side if you encounter pack stock.

- Dispose of your waste properly. This means you pack out what you packed in—including waste, food, and litter. Human waste should be buried 6-8 inches underground and at least 200 feet away from water sources. Toilet paper should be packed out or burned.

- Respect wildlife. Watch wildlife from a distance and don't approach them—there are laws against harassing wildlife. Never feed wildlife and be sure to control your pets when near wild animals.

- Be considerate to others. Keep voices and noises to a minimum and be courteous to other outdoor enthusiasts.

- When four-wheeling, stay on designated roads and trails and do not take shortcuts. Travel during dry weather; going mud-bogging or damaging resources during wet conditions only increases area restrictions and closures.

Outdoor Safety

Outdoor activities are inherently dangerous. You can dramatically reduce your risk of injury or mishap by being prepared, being aware, and using common sense.

- **Be prepared.** In this age of cellular phones, GPS systems, and the availability of search and rescue teams, safety is often taken for granted. Cell phones don't have a reliable connection off the beaten path, especially in the mountains. If they do work, it can still take a considerable amount of time before help can reach your location even if you know exactly where you are. GPS systems can point you in the right direction but won't do the traveling for you. Most survival instructors speak less about actual survival techniques than they do about prevention. Preparing yourself with reliable equipment and the ability to deal with unexpected conditions will serve you well in a time of crisis.

- **Be aware.** This is perhaps the most repeated statement made by safety experts. Situational awareness will allow you to take action before it is too late. Noticing building storm clouds in the morning is better than being alarmed when you first hear a clap of thunder. Noting the mileage on a remote backcountry road is better than suddenly realizing that you have more miles than fuel.

- **Use common sense.** Think before you make decisions. My experience on a search and rescue team has taught me that many emergencies can be prevented with a little forethought.

In terms of safety, there are a few more items that are worth mentioning. Here's an overview, but you are encouraged to learn more on your own.

First Aid

Anybody who recreates in the outdoors should be able to administer general first aid properly. The backcountry is a minefield of potential injuries and dangers. Professional medical services can be hours or even a day or more away depending on conditions and your location. Do you know how to treat an allergic reaction to a sting or handle a sprained ankle? Take the time to learn how to use your first aid kit and learn CPR.

Altitude Sickness

The risk of getting altitude sickness in the Black Hills is low, unless you are acclimated to much lower elevations or have other medical complications. Symptoms include headache, fatigue, nausea, dizziness, and vomiting. To prevent getting these, give your body time to acclimate to higher elevations and drink plenty of water. In general, don't gain more than 7,000 feet of elevation on the first day of your trip. So for example, if you're flying in from the East Coast, you'll be well advised to wait a day or two before visiting the Needles area of the Hills.

Curing altitude sickness in its early phases is simple. Descend from your current elevation and your health should quickly improve.

Drinking Water

Keeping properly hydrated while recreating plays a key role in thwarting many potential illnesses. Most campgrounds have hand-pump wells or piped water. However, some of these water systems are quite dated and can spit out a pretty suspicious-looking liquid even though they are tested annually. To be on the safe side, carry a supply of water with you.

Use special precautions when looking for water in the backcountry. Water from the seemingly purest of sources may pose a risk to your health. The culprits are a variety of bacteria, viruses, parasites, and pollutants. The most commonly reported ailment is Giardiasis, the result of consuming the Giardia parasite, which causes intense diarrhea, vomiting, and cramps. Suitable methods for purifying water include:

- Bring the water to a boil to kill harmful microorganisms. This is undoubtedly the most effective way to treat your drinking water.

- Use iodine tablets. For clear or warm water, use one tablet and wait 10 minutes before drinking. Use two tablets and wait 45 minutes if the water is cold or cloudy. Although simple to use, these tablets lose effectiveness in cold weather and give the water a foul taste.

- Use a water filter or purifier unit. Note that these devices may not neutralize all threats that may be contaminating the water.

Roads and Driving

Many roads in the Black Hills area are dotted with tiny towns, service stations, campgrounds, and businesses—help is nearby if you need it. But other roads, particularly in the national forest, are rugged and remote. These deserve special preparations before driving. The following tips will help ensure a safe trip:

- Keep your vehicle properly maintained, start with a full tank of gas, and carry survival gear with you. Fortunately, as a camper you will already be equipped with supplies such as extra clothing, food, and water. Worth tossing into a bag are jumper cables, a tow rope, and shovel. A compact air compressor and tire repair kit can also be trip savers.

- Keep your speed in check and be alert for other vehicles, ATVs, livestock, and wildlife. If you see wildlife, use a designated turnout or pull completely off the road. Driving excessively slow or stopping in the middle of the road is an invitation for problems.

- Dirt roads can become impassable after a rainstorm. If you are caught on such a road, stay put and let the sun come out for a couple of hours. Attempting to negotiate these troughs of mud during wet conditions can cause you to get stuck or slide off the road. Most storms are short-lived and will quickly pass through the area.

- Remember that at higher elevations, snowdrifts can linger well into late spring and block roads. It's advisable to wait until the snow recedes completely before attempting to blast through a drift, which often conceals a slick layer of ice on the ground.

Off-Road Vehicles

Driving off-road vehicles (ORVs) such as ATVs is permitted and popular on Forest Service roads. Drivers must have either a driver's license or permit to operate on public roads. In Wyoming, ORVs with a muffler and brakes can be driven on Forest Service and BLM roads with a state registration decal. Both states also allow ORVs to be licensed, which allows them to be driven on all public roads except Interstates. ORVs with license plates must also have a horn, rearview mirror, headlights, and a brake light. In South Dakota, ORVs must either have a license plate or a temporary permit, which is common for out-of-state residents. A decal-type of registration may be offered in the future.

When using an ORV, please be respectful of other campers, some of whom are seeking a quiet environment. Remember that ATV riding is not permitted in developed campgrounds unless you are entering or exiting a paid campsite.

Road Conditions and Emergency Contacts

Both Wyoming and South Dakota offer road condition reports that can be accessed online or by phone. For accidents and emergencies, contact local authorities by dialing 911.

Wyoming Road Conditions http://www.wyoroad.info Dial 511 or (888) WYO-ROAD	South Dakota Road Conditions http://www.safetravelusa.com/sd Dial 511

Using this Guide

Each camp write-up includes the following information:

Map

This section shows the page number for the campground's map. The maps and directions included in this book will suffice to get you to the campgrounds, but you're encouraged to carry your own maps. There are many different ways to get to these camps and you may find a shorter, more suitable route.

Usage

The usage section gauges a campground's popularity, a determination that is highly variable. A campground that normally sees little use can have an increase in visitation due to weather, holidays, road construction, local events such as a rally, or closures of neighboring campgrounds. Conversely, a high-use campground may be found nearly empty for reasons ranging from forest fires to an economic recession.

Sites

This section states the number of campsites that are available at the campground.

Cost

Campground rates range from being free to nearly $30 a night. These costs are perpetually changing—increasing and even decreasing—depending on budgets and campground services. On average, expect to pay $10-$20 in addition to any park entrance fees that may apply. Some agencies charge an additional fee for each additional vehicle you have at your site. Some trailheads and picnic areas also have a use fee.

If you are 62 or older, you qualify for a National Parks and Federal Recreational Lands Pass – Senior Pass. After an initial $10 fee, this lifetime pass permits free entrance to any national park, monument, or federal recreation area in the United States. It is also good for a 50% discount on most recreation sites like campgrounds and trailheads. The free Access Pass has similar benefits, but is offered to permanently disabled U.S. citizens. You can get these passports at federal recreation sites and offices by calling (888) 275-8747 or by visiting http://store.usgs.gov/pass.

If you are looking for free camping, you have several options:

- Find a dispersed campsite or a remote campground that doesn't charge fees.
- Camp in a Wyoming Game & Fish recreation area.
- Camp in the off-season when some campgrounds are free.

Facilities
Campgrounds can have a variety of facilities such as fire rings, grills, picnic tables, water, showers, pit toilets, restrooms, trash containers, playgrounds, amphitheaters, RV dump stations, laundry facilities, and pay phones. It's important to note that the availability of facilities are not always reliable. The presence of trash containers, for instance, seems to depend on an agency's recreation budget. The availability of potable water is even more unpredictable. It is not uncommon for a campground's water well, or tap, to be shut down if the water doesn't meet health standards, the weather is cold, or the system is undergoing maintenance. Consider carrying at least one gallon of water with you at all times.

Spur Length
This section gives a general guideline to the length of the parking spur where you'll park your car, RV, or trailer. These are general lengths, not actual measurements. In most cases with a trailer, your tow vehicle will have to be unhitched in order to fit. The lengths of the parking spurs are defined as follows:

- Short: Under 30 feet (best for tent campers or short pop-up trailers)
- Medium: 30-40 feet (may be able to fit larger trailers or motorhomes into the spot, depending on the site)
- Long: Over 40 feet (suitable for any type of RV or trailer)

Managing Agency
Agencies that maintain public campgrounds throughout the Black Hills include the National Park Service, USDA Forest Service, Wyoming Game & Fish Department, Wyoming State Parks, South Dakota Game, Fish, and Parks, the US Army Corps of Engineers, and the city of Spearfish. Some campgrounds have a volunteer or paid host who maintains the camp facilities. Hosts can vary by year, but this section notes if one is often present.

Reservations

This section includes reservation information, if applicable. Reservations can be made from these sources:

Federal Agencies (National Park Service, Forest Service)
www.recreation.gov
(877) 444-6777

South Dakota State Parks
www.campsd.com
(800) 710-2267

Wyoming State Parks
www.wyo-park.com
(877) 996-7275

Campgrounds in Wyoming's Black Hills mostly operate on a first-come, first-served basis. While some do accept reservations, these are often unnecessary. On the other hand, reservations are recommended, even required, for many of the campgrounds in South Dakota. If you don't have reservations, your best chance for getting a good campsite is to arrive at the campground between 9:00 a.m. and 3:00 p.m. to secure a vacated, unclaimed site.

Season

This section gives a campground's normal operating season. Many of the campgrounds are open between Memorial Day weekend and Labor Day weekend. There may be a great departure from this time frame depending on a campground's location, elevation, and the season's weather. Cold temperatures or maintenance can keep a campground closed for weeks after the planned opening date. When planning a trip, keep in mind that opening dates are more tentative than the closing dates. It is also not quite as busy at the beginning of the season than towards the end.

While you will be able to get into some campgrounds during the off-season, some are physically barricaded by lock and gate. Others are only accessible by snowmobile. If you are planning an off-season camping trip, check with the governing agency to confirm that you'll have access to the area. If you do, you'll enjoy several benefits of off-season camping. For one, unless it's hunting season, you'll be able to take the site of your choice. Second, fire restrictions from the dry, hot summer months are usually lifted in the spring and fall. Third, by staying in a campground that hasn't been officially opened (or has closed) for the season and doesn't yet offer services, your site will usually be free or have a reduced rate. Just remember to take plenty of water, pack out your own trash, and leave your site as you found it (or better).

Elevation

This section shows the campground's elevation from sea level, in feet. Camps at lower elevations tend to be warmer, drier, and have fewer trees. Camps at higher elevations are often cooler, more heavily timbered, and receive more precipitation.

GPS Coordinates

Geographic coordinates are provided for each campground. These coordinates are in the degrees, decimal minutes format. If you need a different format, you'll find many coordinate converter websites on the Internet.

Take note that the coordinates may not be as precise as you expect. Variances between GPS receivers, satellite reception, and mapping software can plot the coordinates a short distance from the intended point. Commonly, this difference is only a few yards but you may encounter others that are off by a quarter mile.

Description

Each campground write-up describes campsites with information relating to privacy, room, shade, popularity, and local features.

Field Notes

This section includes additional notes about the campground or area and may include my personal opinion, field observations, or other general notes.

Directions

This section includes driving directions for each campground. Mileage reported on your tripometer may vary slightly. US and State highways are abbreviated as "HWY." Interstates are abbreviated with an "I" and "FR" and "CR" refer to Forest Road and County Road respectively.

The maps shown in this book are intended for general navigation only. For simplicity, these maps show the basics—you'll find them helpful for locating campgrounds, but for other recreation purposes get a detailed local map. Depending on your activities, you may need to consult several different maps; more than a dozen were used to find all the information included in this book.

Detailed maps of national and state parks are available at their entrance stations. If you are traveling into the Black Hills National Forest, consider buying a forest map so that you can find your way along the hundreds of miles of backroads. While most Forest Service roads are adequately marked, signs can fall, fade, rot, get stolen, or be vandalized. Keeping your bearings on a map is the best way to navigate the national forest.

Getting Started

The campgrounds in this book are separated into three chapters, as shown below. Within each area, campgrounds are generally listed from north to south or from east to west, although they are sometimes grouped in the order that you are likely to drive past them. If you don't know yet where you're headed, this will get you started:

Northern Black Hills
Page 27 This chapter includes campgrounds that are north of Hill City, South Dakota.

Southern Black Hills
Page 79 This chapter includes campgrounds that are south of Hill City, South Dakota. It includes Badlands National Park, which is southwest of Rapid City.

Wyoming's Black Hills
Page 145 The rumors are true—the Black Hills are in Wyoming too. This chapter describes the campgrounds found in and near the Hills of northeastern Wyoming.

Popular Attractions
Page 163 Black Hills country is full of museums, scenic attractions, tourist traps, amusement parks... you name it. Many of these attractions are described in local travel magazines or tourism brochures, but this section gives you a concise summary of the most popular destinations.

Contacts
Page 171 Ready to go? Have a specific question? Here is who you need to contact before you head out the door.

NORTHERN BLACK HILLS
CAMPGROUNDS NORTH OF HILL CITY

The northern half of the Black Hills—the area north of Hill City—is a regional hub for outdoor recreation. Long backcountry paths like the Centennial Trail, Deerfield Trail, and George S. Mickelson Trail bring hikers, mountain bikers, and horseback riders. Backcountry drivers and ATV riders kick up dust on hundreds of miles of dirt roads. The towering rock walls of Spearfish Canyon, and the waterfalls that cascade between them, bring sightseers of all ages and abilities. Then there is the camping with water sports. Of the nearly two dozen campgrounds in this area, more than half of them are at a lake or reservoir. Most of the rest are along a stream or spring. With access to this much water, it's no surprise that boating, fishing, and swimming are popular activities here.

Outside of outdoor recreation, the northern Black Hills offer visitors plenty to do. First and foremost is the massive motorcycle rally that draws hundreds of thousands of people to the town of Sturgis (and the entire region) each August. There are numerous visitor centers and museums where you can spend hours or even a whole day. One of the larger attractions is the Minuteman Missile National Historic Site east of Rapid City where you can discover the powerful missiles that kept the peace during the Cold War. Wall Drug and its many rooms of food, souvenirs, and other merchandise can keep you entertained for longer than you planned. The same can be said about the casinos in Deadwood. Regardless of your pursuit, you'll likely find it here.

Northern Black Hills Campgrounds

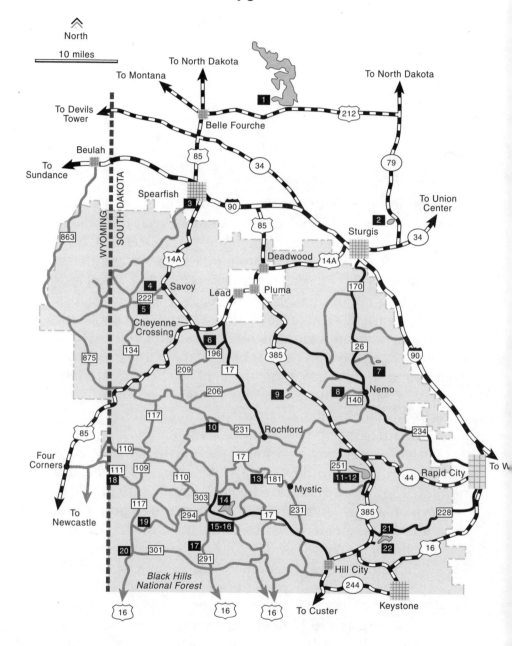

North

10 miles

To North Dakota

To Montana

To Devils Tower

Beulah

To Sundance

WYOMING

SOUTH DAKOTA

Spearfish

Belle Fourche

To North Dakota

212

85

34

79

90

85

863

14A

Savoy

Deadwood

14A

Sturgis

34

To Union Center

170

4

222

5

Lead

Pluma

Cheyenne Crossing

6

196

134

385

26

7

90

875

209

17

206

9

8

140

Nemo

85

117

10

231

Rochford

234

Four Corners

110

17

111

109

251

11-12

44

Rapid City

To W

18

110

13

181

Mystic

385

228

117

303

14

231

19

294

17

21

To Newcastle

15-16

22

16

20

301

17

291

Black Hills National Forest

Hill City

244

Keystone

To Custer

16

16

16

1

2

3

Campground Number	Campground Name	Page Number
1	Rocky Point Recreation Area Campground	30
2	Bear Butte State Park Campgrounds	33
3	Spearfish City Campground	35
4	Rod and Gun Campground	37
5	Timon Campground	39
6	Hanna Campground	41
7	Dalton Lake Campground	43
8	Boxelder Forks Campground	45
9	Roubaix Lake Campground	47
10	Black Fox Campground	49
11	Pactola Campground	52
12	Bear Gulch Group Campground	54
13	Castle Peak Campground	56
14	Custer Trail Campground (Deerfield Reservoir)	59
15	Dutchman Campground (Deerfield Reservoir)	61
16	Whitetail Campground (Deerfield Reservoir)	63
17	Ditch Creek Campground	65
18	Beaver Creek Campground	67
19	Redbank Springs Campground	69
20	Moon Campground	71
21	Sheridan North Cove Group Campground	73
22	Sheridan Lake Southside Campground	75

Rocky Point Recreation Area

Opened in 2006, Rocky Point Recreation Area is a modern state park that features the 8,000-acre Belle Fourche Reservoir. Located 8 miles east of the rural town of Belle Fourche, this recreation site is a good distance from the busy Black Hills, which can be seen across the horizon. Out here, the sky is as big as it gets, and you'll enjoy panoramic sunrises and sunsets across the water.

1 Rocky Point Recreation Area Campground
Lakeside camping north of the Black Hills

Map	Page 28
Usage	Moderate
Sites	61
Cost	$14 ($18 for electric). A daily park entrance fee or annual pass is also required.
Camp Facilities	Fire rings, sheltered picnic tables, water, restrooms, showers, trash containers, boat ramp, playground, fish cleaning station, dump station, picnic shelter
Spur Length	Long—up to 85 feet
Managing Agency	South Dakota Game, Fish and Parks; a host is on site
Reservations	Accepted—check www.campsd.com or call (800) 710-2267
Season	Open all year
Elevation	3,000 feet
GPS Coordinates	N44° 42.81' W103° 42.16'

The Camp

This state park is a prime example of South Dakota not holding back when it comes to their recreation sites—they take the primitive aspects out of camping. To start, there are electric hookups, flush toilets, and showers. You'll find a playground with children's equipment and horseshoe pits. A couple other facilities, a fish cleaning station and a dump station, simply make camp life more convenient. Recreationally, there is a shop that rents kayaks and even a designated shore fishing area if you choose not to fish from a boat. The fish that swim these waters include catfish, smallmouth and white bass, tigermuskie, walleye, yellow perch, and black crappie.

This is flat and open prairie land—the paved roads that lead to and through the park couldn't be easier to drive. Those hauling cumbersome RVs or trailers will have no trouble parking their rigs on the long, level parking spurs.

The entire recreation site occupies a peninsula on the reservoir. All of the regular campsites are lined along the northern and western half of this area. The lion's share of these face the reservoir's lightly-timbered shoreline, which is just a short walking distance from the parking spurs. The eastern half of the area features the fishing area, boat ramps, and a picnic shelter. On the southern end, you'll find five group sites—signed A through E— that are big gravel spurs. These sites accommodate up to five tents (only two vehicles permitted, though) and no electric hookups.

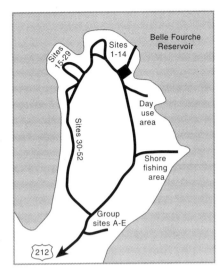

Though deciduous trees line the shore, there is no shade at the campsites. The temperature heats up here, so the early and late weeks of summer make ideal times to visit. Of course, if you're planning to spend your time on the water, the dog days of summer may just be the perfect time.

Rocky Point Recreation Area

Field Notes

I spent a weekend here in September and found only a handful of campers, most from Montana. The camp was quiet with only a breeze creating a stir.

Directions

From I-90 at Spearfish, take Exit 10 and drive north on HWY 85 for 10.5 miles to the north end of Belle Fourche. Turn east on HWY 212 and drive 7 miles to the park on the left. You can also reach the park from I-90 at Sturgis. Take Exit 30 and follow HWY 34 east for 5 miles to HWY 79. Turn north and drive 18.7 miles to HWY 212. Turn west and drive a final 15.2 miles.

Bear Butte State Park

Bear Butte State Park is characterized by a nearly 1,000-foot igneous rock intrusion that rises dramatically from the surrounding plains to top 4,426 feet. The Lakota named this mount Mato Paha, or Bear Mountain. It's a sacred place for many American Indians, and the site is still used for religious ceremonies.

State Highway 79 bisects the state park and splits it into two distinct areas. On the east side, you'll find the butte and an education center. You may also spot bison that roam around the base of the mountain. On the west side of the highway, there is Bear Butte Lake with two miles of shoreline and three camping areas.

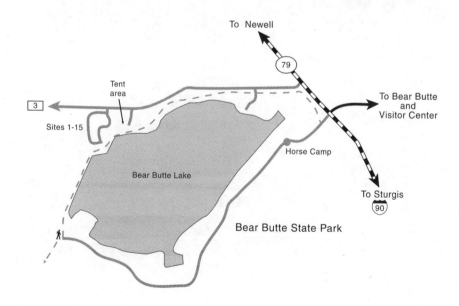

Mount Rushmore
National Memorial.

Roughlock Falls
Nature Area
near Spearfish,
South Dakota.

NORTHERN BLACK HILLS

Bear Gulch at Pactola Reservoir.

Rod and Gun Campground.

Deerfield Lake.

SOUTHERN BLACK HILLS

Bismark Lake.

The Needles.

Needles Highway.

Harney Peak.

Custer State Park.

Badlands National Park.

WYOMING'S BLACK HILLS

Cook Lake
Campground.

Devils Tower
National
Monument.

2 Bear Butte State Park Campgrounds
Plains camping near Sturgis and I-90

Map	Page 28, 32
Usage	Moderate
Sites	15+ sites; 4 horse sites
Cost	$10; $12 horse site. A daily park entrance fee or annual pass is also required.
Camp Facilities	Fire rings, picnic tables, water, pit toilets, trash containers, group picnic shelter
Spur Length	Long—up to 60 feet
Managing Agency	South Dakota Game, Fish and Parks; a host is on site
Reservations	Not accepted—first come, first served
Season	Open all year
Elevation	3,200 feet
GPS Coordinates	N44° 27.56' W103° 27.08'

The Camps
Bear Butte State Park is located 7 miles northeast of Sturgis, making it one of the easiest public camping areas to reach from I-90. Any campground with a mountain, a lake, and highway access is almost always busy. Still, this is a fairly sleepy place for most of the year, but not during August when the Sturgis motorcycle rally is underway.

Bear Butte State Park

The state park has three camping areas. The first is on the east side of Bear Butte Lake, near the highway. This is a four-site horse camp—really just a parking lot—with a small corral. This is simple camping with water, a pit toilet, and a few picnic tables. There are no shade trees here, and summertime temperatures can get hot. Horseback riders can ride westward from the camp on the Centennial Trail or ride around the lake. No riding is allowed on the east side of the highway. From the camp, there is a narrow gravel lane that wraps around the southern shore of the lake.

The park's main campground is found on the other side of the lake, about a mile from the highway. Here, you'll find long parking spurs that will easily accommodate long RVs, though some will require leveling. The camp's sprawling grassy lawn is ideal for tents and gives the camp a roomy feel. There are a few trees scattered around the campground, though most are too small to provide shade. Some sites include a shelter over the picnic tables, others don't. A large covered picnic shelter is also located here in the campground as is a fishing dock near the lake.

A separate tent area with another few sites is located just east of the main camp and offers campers closer proximity to the water. These sites are covered by large deciduous trees, making them the most shaded out of all the campsites.

For a recreation site that is mostly on the plains, Bear Butte State Park is rich with hiking trails. The most exciting route is the Summit Trail—a designated National Recreation Trail—that takes you 1.85 miles to the top of Bear Butte. This is a moderate hike that begins near the education center. Closer to camp, you'll find the Lake Trail. This is a grassy track that wraps 2.5 miles around Bear Butte Lake. Then there is the Centennial Trail, a 111-mile path that starts here in the park (technically at the top of the butte) and heads southward through the Black Hills to terminate at Wind Cave National Park. From the Bear Butte Lake Trailhead (at the west end of the lake), it is 4.5 miles southward to reach the Ft. Meade Trailhead, which is just one of nearly two dozen designated access points.

Anglers will find crappie, bullheads, and northern pike in the lake. There have also been reports of catfish and yellow perch. Boats with motors smaller than 25 horsepower are allowed on these waters.

Field Notes
Whether you're out hiking, fishing, or just playing around camp, remember to watch for rattlesnakes and bison.

Directions
From I-90 at Sturgis, take Exit 30 and follow HWY 34 east for 5 miles to HWY 79. Turn north and drive 3 miles.

Spearfish City Campground
3 City park camping at the edge of town

Map	Page 28
Usage	Moderate to high
Sites	62 hook-up sites; 150 primitive sites
Cost	$18-$34 ($10 during the off season)
Camp Facilities	Fire rings, grills, picnic tables, water, electric/cable/sewer hookups, restrooms, showers, Internet access, dump station, pay phones, vending machines, trash containers
Spur Length	Long—up to 50 feet
Managing Agency	Spearfish Parks and Recreation
Reservations	Accepted—call (605) 642-1340
Season	Open all year (hookups and facilities available May through September)
Elevation	3,700 feet
GPS Coordinates	N44° 28.81' W103° 51.57'

The Camp

Located on the south side of Spearfish next to the Black Hills National Forest is Spearfish City Campground, a camp operated by the city that offers the best of both the urban and backcountry environments. Here, you'll find grassy lawns where you can kick back and surf the web, watch cable TV, or head to a nearby restaurant. But don't think of this camp as being squashed between storefronts. Rather, it's tucked away from the busy

Spearfish City Campground

streets in a mixed forest of both evergreen and deciduous trees. Spearfish Creek and one of its tributaries flows through the camp and deer are frequent visitors. From here, you have quick access to I-90 if you're headed elsewhere (say Sturgis or Yellowstone), as well as the Spearfish Canyon Scenic Byway, if you're headed to the Black Hills high country.

The campsites offer a tiered level of comfort. Near the park office, you'll find a handful of what are called premium sites. These have full hookups and generous spacing next to the scenic stream. Spaced out along a couple of paved roads are another 56 sites with full hookups. These are squeezed tightly together with only a few feet between their gravel parking spurs. They are also much shorter—many will only accommodate short pop-up trailers or pickup campers if you're bringing an RV. The south and west side of the campground has 150 primitive sites, which are basically fire rings scattered about the lush grassy lawn.

The cost of the campground is also tiered and depends not only on the site you choose, but when you choose it. If you're staying here during the Sturgis motorcycle rally, be prepared to pay $40 to $60 per night. If you're here during the off-season, you'll only pay $10. Depending on the site you choose, you may also be charged for each additional person in your group. There is no charge for children five years and younger.

Field Notes

Staying this close to town has its benefits. If it's a sunny day, you can head up into the Hills or take advantage of the recreational path that cuts through the camp. If the weather has you hunkered down, you can spend your day in town or tour the D.C. Booth Historic National Fish Hatchery, which is just across from the park.

Directions

From I-90 at Spearfish, take Exit 12 and drive west for .7 miles to Canyon Street. Turn left and drive south for another .7 miles to the Spearfish City Park. You can also reach the camp by taking Exit 14. Follow Colorado Boulevard westward for 1.5 miles and turn left onto HWY 14A. Drive south for less than a half mile and turn right onto Winterville Drive. Follow this road to Canyon Street and then turn right and drive a short distance to the campground.

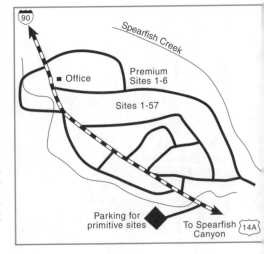

Rod and Gun Campground
4
Rocky camp in Spearfish Canyon

Map	Page 28
Usage	Moderate
Sites	7
Cost	$15 ($10 during the off season)
Camp Facilities	Fire rings, picnic tables, water, pit toilets, trash containers
Spur Length	Long—up to 50 feet
Managing Agency	USDA Forest Service—Black Hills National Forest
Reservations	Not accepted—first come, first served
Season	Open April through November
Elevation	5,375 feet
GPS Coordinates	N44° 20.32' W103° 57.84'

The Camp
Rod and Gun is among the Black Hills' most scenic campgrounds. Situated below the cliffs and towering outcrops of Spearfish Canyon, this camp is close to some of South Dakota's most well-known attractions such as Roughlock Falls and the Spearfish Canyon Scenic Byway. Locals also like

Rod and Gun Campground

to point out that part of the 1990 movie, Dances with Wolves, was filmed in this canyon.

The camp has half a dozen sites spaced along a single lane against the brushy base of a canyon wall. The last site—the most private—is found in the turnaround at the far end of the lane. Trees are shorter and scarcer here, so most sites are sunny with little privacy. Not all the parking spurs are long enough to easily accommodate large trailers, so those with tents or small trailers hold an advantage. Surprisingly, the campground doesn't get crowded too often, though there is heavy traffic along the main road from tourists.

Little Spearfish Creek flows between the campsites and the main road and holds brook trout. The Rimrock Trail, a footpath, can be found running through the camp along the creek. This is an 8-mile trail that includes a lower loop, which can be started here, or an upper loop, which can be accessed from Timon Campground farther up the road.

Field Notes
September is a terrific time to camp in this canyon because the flora is bright with autumn colors and the temperatures are mild. If you visit during the summer and find the camp full, or you want more shade or a longer parking spur, drive west for 1.7 miles to Timon Campground.

Directions
From I-90 at Spearfish, take HWY 14A (Spearfish Canyon Scenic Byway) southward for 13 miles to Savoy. Turn right onto FR 222 and drive 3 miles to the camp on the right.

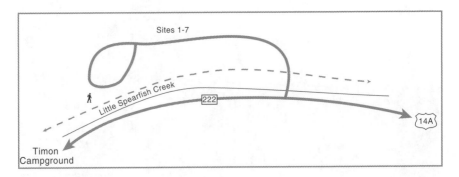

5 Timon Campground
Timbered camp in the upper reaches of Spearfish Canyon

Map	Page 28
Usage	Low to moderate
Sites	7
Cost	$15 ($10 during the off season)
Camp Facilities	Fire rings, picnic tables, water, pit toilets, trash containers
Spur Length	Long—up to 40 feet
Managing Agency	USDA Forest Service—Black Hills National Forest
Reservations	Not accepted—first come, first served
Season	Open April through November
Elevation	5,600 feet
GPS Coordinates	N44° 19.71' W103° 59.3'

The Camp
Timon Campground is located where the narrow, steep walls of Spearfish Canyon begin to widen into gentler and more forested terrain. The shrubs, brambles, and deciduous trees of the lower canyon are replaced here by mature spruce trees that cast shadows across the camp. If it's the summer heat you're trying to escape, Timon will best nearby Rod and Gun Campground.

Timon Campground

The campsites are spaced on both the inside and outside of a compact loop. The four outside spurs are the most spacious, while the three interior spurs can feel crowded. Although the camp is sloped, there are some long, level spurs and plenty of nice grass for tents. Little Spearfish Creek runs past the camp, parallel to the main road.

If you want to explore this scenic area on foot, there are several trails from which you can choose. The Rimrock Trail is an 8-mile path that includes an upper loop, starting here at the campground, and a lower loop, which can be accessed from nearby Rod and Gun Campground. Another option is the Little Spearfish Trail, a 5.7-mile loop that also starts from the camp. This trail can be used to access a walk-in fishing area that is found to the southwest.

To reach a scenic overlook of this area, grab a Black Hills National Forest map and follow FR 222, FR 105, FR 804, and FR 850 westward for about 8 miles to reach the Cement Ridge Lookout in nearby Wyoming. The drive is fun—a bit rocky near the top—and the sweeping views are worthwhile.

Field Notes

I'm surprised how little use this camp receives at times. On a perfect late summer weekend, nearby Roughlock Falls was so crowded that cars were lined up waiting for a parking spot. At this camp, however, only one site was occupied. Drive-by traffic is high but few stay.

Directions

From I-90 at Spearfish, take HWY 14A (Spearfish Canyon Scenic Byway) southward for 13 miles to Savoy. Turn right onto FR 222 and drive 4.6 miles to the camp on the left.

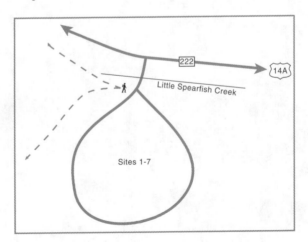

Hanna Campground
Quiet camp near Spearfish Canyon

Map	Page 28
Usage	Moderate
Sites	13
Cost	$15
Camp Facilities	Fire rings, picnic tables, water, pit toilets
Spur Length	Long—up to 55 feet
Managing Agency	USDA Forest Service—Black Hills National Forest; a host is on site
Reservations	Not accepted—first come, first served
Season	Late May to early September (walk-in sites open all year)
Elevation	5,600 feet
GPS Coordinates	N44° 16.47' W103° 51.05'

The Camp

Hanna Campground is a quite alternative to the busier camps located in the northern Black Hills. Reached from paved roads near Spearfish Canyon, you can quickly escape the sightseeing crowds and settle in for the night. East Spearfish Creek—one of the larger streams you'll find in the Black

Hanna Campground

Hills—flows between the campsites and the road. This timbered waterway helps create some separation between your site and passing traffic.

The camp arrangement is quite unique. On the left side, there are seven long, level spurs that will accommodate about anything you could drive here. These are treeless sites that occupy just a small part of a large sloping meadow. To the right, you'll find a trail that leads to six walk-in tent sites, some of which are situated around a stand of spruce. If you choose one of the walk-in sites, park in one of the two designated tent parking areas along the main road, and then use the footbridges to carry your gear over the creek and to your site.

Large groups will love the open grassy area, as will kids who like to run off their energy. For day trips away from camp, head north 2 miles to reach the Spearfish Canyon Scenic Byway (HWY 14A). There are numerous designated picnic areas along the byway and its peripheral roads. The most popular nearby attraction is Roughlock Falls—a beautiful cascade along an interpretive trail—located 5 miles north of Cheyenne Crossing.

Field Notes
If you don't need a lot of shade, you'll like it here. This is a nice camp, especially on those days when temperatures are mild.

Directions
From I-90 at Spearfish, take HWY 14A (Spearfish Canyon Scenic Byway) southward for 18.5 miles to HWY 85 at Cheyenne Crossing. (You can also reach this point from Lead by taking HWY 85 south for 8 miles.) From this junction, turn right and drive west for a tenth of a mile before turning left onto FR 196. Follow this paved road southward for 2.2 miles to reach the camp.

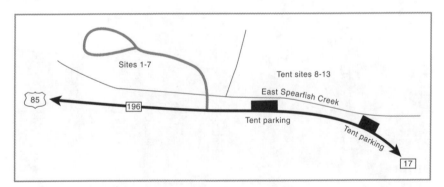

7 Dalton Lake Campground
A hidden camp at the local fishing hole

Map	Page 28
Usage	Moderate
Sites	11
Cost	$15
Camp Facilities	Fire rings, picnic tables, water, pit toilets, trash containers
Spur Length	Long—up to 45 feet
Managing Agency	USDA Forest Service—Black Hills National Forest; a host is on site
Reservations	Not accepted—first come, first served
Season	Late May to early September
Elevation	4,400 feet
GPS Coordinates	N44° 13.78' W103° 28.63'

The Camp

Dalton Lake Campground is a nicely maintained camp next to a small lake in the northeastern Black Hills. Tall spruce and ponderosa pines provide plenty of shade to help moderate temperatures at this relatively low elevation.

Dalton Lake

The first few sites are reserved for picnicking and the camp host. The remaining parking spurs are level and nicely spaced along a narrow gravel lane. Most of these are on the same side as Dalton Lake, which is within a few paces. On the other end of camp, you'll find a covered picnic area complete with an old brick fireplace.

Dalton Lake itself is a small, slender body of water fed and drained by Elk Creek. The camp side of the lake has a handicap-accessible path with walkouts that take you out over the shoreline. Trout fishing is common and there is a separate day-use parking area that anglers can use.

Peaceful weekdays often give way to a busier, louder weekend as traffic increases and folks come here to camp, fish, picnic, and just drive through the area. The Centennial Trail—the 111-mile long path that traverses the Black Hills—is nearby and you'll find access at Dalton Trailhead, just a short distance past the camp. You can expect some ATV traffic in this area as well.

Field Notes

The incoming road to this camp is narrow and choked with dense brush that provides good cover for wildlife. When I made a trip here on a quiet fall day, I spotted a bobcat right on the road. It tolerated my presence for just a few seconds before jumping into the roadside brush where it was impossible to watch.

Directions

From I-90 at Sturgis, take Exit 32 and turn south onto Vanocker Canyon Road, which turns into FR 26. Drive south on this paved steep road for about 13 miles. Turn left onto FR 224 and follow this narrow road for 4 miles to the camp.

If coming from Rapid City, you can take Nemo Road (CR 234), shown on some maps as South Canyon Road, for 19 miles to Nemo. Continue another half mile to the north and then bear right onto FR 26. Drive north on this paved road for 3.5 miles and turn right onto FR 224. Follow this narrow lane for 4 miles to the campground.

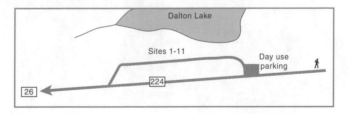

8 Boxelder Forks Campground
Secluded campground with easy access

Map	Page 28
Usage	Low to moderate
Sites	14
Cost	$15 (no fee during the off season)
Camp Facilities	Fire rings, picnic tables, water, pit toilets, trash containers
Spur Length	USDA Forest Service—Black Hills National Forest; a host is on site
Managing Agency	Long—up to 45 feet
Reservations	Not accepted—first come, first served
Season	Open all year
Elevation	4,700 feet
GPS Coordinates	N44° 11.86' W103° 32.13'

The Camp

If you're looking for an out-of-the-way camp but don't want to bounce along many miles of dirt backroads to reach it, Boxelder Forks is for you. Tall spruce and ponderosa pines shade a grassy park with spacious campsites that have long spurs. Boxelder Creek runs beside the camp and

Boxelder Forks Campground

half of the sites are along the water. A tributary of this stream divides the campground into two areas that are connected by a footbridge. The first sites you encounter, 12-14, are situated along the main road, so they receive more noise and dust. These three sites are the only ones that are open during the off-season months. The remaining sites, 1 through 11, are tucked away and quieter.

The incoming road offers a few worthwhile features, including a scenic and rocky canyon along Boxelder Creek. You'll also pass Boxelder Creek Trailhead, which is an access point for the Black Hills' longest track, the 111-mile long Centennial Trail (Trail 89). The section of the trail that passes through here (between Pilot Knob and Dalton) is the only stretch where some motorized use is allowed, so ATV riding is common. You may also encounter horseback riders as well. The nearby restaurant and bar in Nemo is a popular congregating spot for recreationists.

Field Notes

This camp is a personal favorite—it's a peaceful refuge in a national forest that buzzes with summertime activity. The forest is especially full and beautiful around the camp, so it's no wonder the national Christmas tree was taken near here in 1970. It wasn't easy getting the 78-foot spruce to Washington, however. The train that carried it eastward was twice derailed in neighboring Nebraska.

Directions

From I-90 east of Spearfish, take Exit 17 and turn onto HWY 85. Drive south for 10.5 miles to reach HWY 385 at Pluma (just south of Deadwood). Turn onto HWY 385 and continue south for nearly 8 miles. Turn left onto paved Nemo Road and follow it for 13 miles to Nemo. Turn right onto FR 140 and drive west for 1.9 miles. You'll pass three campsites on the right before reaching the main campground entrance near a bridge.

If coming from Rapid City, you can take Nemo Road (CR 234), shown on some maps as South Canyon Road, for 19 miles to Nemo. Then turn left onto FR 140 and drive 1.9 miles to the camp on the right.

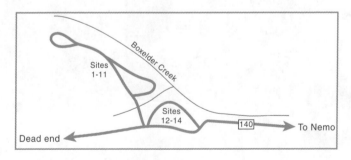

9 Roubaix Lake Campground
Lake camping in the north central Black Hills

Map	Page 28
Usage	High
Sites	57
Cost	$19 ($10 during the off season)
Camp Facilities	Fire rings, picnic tables, water, pit toilets, trash containers
Spur Length	Long—up to 45 feet
Managing Agency	USDA Forest Service—Black Hills National Forest; a host is on site
Reservations	Accepted—check www.recreation.gov or call (877) 444-6777
Season	Open all year (13 sites remain open in the off season)
Elevation	5,500 feet
GPS Coordinates	N44° 11.95' W103° 39.66'

The Camp

Roubaix Lake (pronounced roo-bey) is a small but busy lake in the northern Black Hills that appeals to water lovers. On the camp side of the lake, you'll find a sandy swim beach. Nearby is a footbridge that spans the northern outlet so that you can reach the far shoreline. Non-motorized boat access expands the trout fishing opportunities here while maintaining calm and quiet waters. There is no boat ramp, so you'll need a craft that you can carry.

Roubaix Lake

The campground is comprised of four loops that are situated in a pine forest north and west of the lake. This is monotonous looking woodland, void of much understory or firewood pickings, but it does offer plenty of shade. Sites 1-9 are found in Loop A, closest to the camp's entrance and furthest from the lake. The next ten sites in Loop B are a little closer and a footpath leads down to the lake's main parking lot. Most of the 18 sites in and next to Loop C are the noisiest—these are the closest to the lake and drivers come past them to reach the main parking lot. Loop D holds the last 20 sites and these receive the least amount of drive-through traffic.

All campsites and parking spurs are not equal here; some are standard, while others are designated only for tents. Some sites are reservable and others are assigned to campers upon arrival. To ensure you get the spot you want, especially if you're camping on a busy holiday weekend, be sure to make a reservation.

Field Notes
By the middle of September, this is a quiet place. On one late summer visit, I found just one camper in the only loop that remained open. A few cars came and went in the short afternoon hours, but the recreation area fell silent when night fell.

Directions
From I-90 east of Spearfish, take Exit 17 and turn onto HWY 85. Drive south for 10.5 miles to reach HWY 385 at Pluma (just south of Deadwood). Turn onto HWY 385 and continue south for 13.5 miles. Turn right onto the access road and follow it west for 1 mile.

If coming from Rapid City, take HWY 44 west for 17 miles. Turn right onto HWY 385 and drive north for 10.5 miles. Turn left and drive 1 mile.

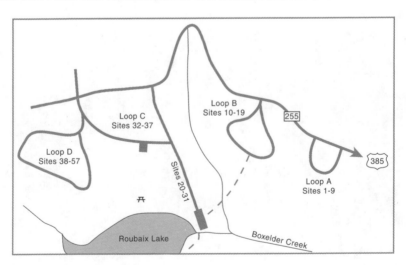

10 Black Fox Campground
Roadside camping in the lonely central Black Hills

Map	Page 28
Usage	Low
Sites	9
Cost	None
Camp Facilities	Fire rings, picnic tables, pit toilets
Spur Length	Long—up to 45 feet
Managing Agency	USDA Forest Service—Black Hills National Forest
Reservations	Not accepted—first come, first served
Season	Open all year (snowmobile access from December through March)
Elevation	5,900 feet
GPS Coordinates	N44° 8.7' W103° 50.71'

The Camp

This remote camp can offer complete solitude, unless a car rumbles down the gravel road within a few feet of your campsite. Three of the sites sit directly along the main road, collecting dust whenever someone passes by. Others sit just slightly further back. The east side of the camp is bound by Rhoades Fork Creek, which flows into South Fork Rapid Creek just north of the camp (and it is indeed rapid). These streams are the camp's main attraction, and anglers can take small trout from them.

Black Fox Campground

Trees are few along the road, but mature spruce do provide a nice canopy over some of the sites. The pit toilet is found on the opposite side of the road behind an unnumbered site.

Field Notes
Over the course of the hour or two that I spent here on a sunny, summer day, only two cars passed by the camp. Still, if you are camping with small children, the close proximity of the sites to the road could be troublesome.

Directions
From Spearfish, take HWY 14A (Spearfish Canyon Scenic Byway) southward for 18.5 miles to HWY 85 at Cheyenne Crossing. From this junction, turn left and drive east for just over 4 miles to reach paved FR 17. (You can reach this same point from Lead by taking HWY 85 southward for 3.5 miles). Now drive south for 15 miles to Rochford. Turn right and drive west on FR 231 for 8 miles. Turn left onto FR 233 to find the campground entrance.

There are many other ways to get to this campground. Check a Black Hills National Forest map to find the route that best suits you.

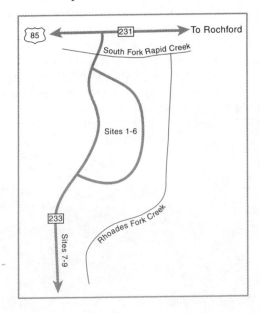

Pactola Reservoir

Pactola was a small gold rush town that occupied a mountain valley in the Black Hills. In addition to the settlement, there were church camps, a camp for the Civilian Conservation Corps (CCC), and a center for tuberculosis patients. These sites are now at the bottom of Pactola Reservoir, the largest and deepest lake in the mountainous Black Hills.

Construction on the 230-foot high and 1,255-foot wide dam structure began in late 1952 and was completed during the summer of 1956. It created an 800-acre lake that is 150 feet deep and has 14 miles of shoreline. Today, the Bureau of Reclamation manages the dam and reservoir. The water is used for irrigation, recreation, flood control, and municipal use.

Pactola Reservoir is very popular, in part because it's so accessible and visible. Highway 385 cuts directly over the dam, revealing glorious views over the water that beckon your camera from its case. There is an overlook pull-off and Forest Service visitor center on the south end of the dam that is open during the peak summer season.

There are two campgrounds at Pactola and both are on the south side of the reservoir. One is Bear Gulch, a remote group campground. The main one, Pactola, is a sprawling recreation site that accommodates hundreds of campers in a rolling ponderosa pine forest.

Pactola Reservoir

11 Pactola Campground
A recreational playground on the shore of a large reservoir

Map	Page 28
Usage	High
Sites	88
Cost	$16-$21 (no fee during the off season)
Camp Facilities	Fire rings, grills, picnic tables, water, restrooms, trash containers, boat ramp
Spur Length	Long—up to 50 feet
Managing Agency	USDA Forest Service—Black Hills National Forest; a host is on site
Reservations	Accepted—check www.recreation.gov or call (877) 444-6777
Season	Open all year
Elevation	4,800 feet
GPS Coordinates	N44° 3.92' W103° 30.20'

The Camp
Pactola Campground has three separate loops that seem to be out of order. The first is Loop C, which contains the first 22 sites in addition to 8 terrific tent sites. This loop receives the most traffic because it offers a direct route to the reservoir and boat ramp. Sites 23-47 are found in Loop A, which is the middle section of the campground. The last, Loop B, contains sites 48-80 and is the furthest from the water.

Pactola Campground

Among the loops, there are four handicap-accessible sites. Many of the campsites have a limited view of the water. Long parking spurs accommodate large RVs and trailers.

The reservoir is a well-known fishery in this part of South Dakota. Famed for its record lake trout—a 28 pounder was caught in 2009—the waters also hold perch, rainbow trout, and brown trout. Fishing for sizable brown trout is also popular in Rapid Creek, above and below the lake. East of the campground, you'll find the reservoir's southern marina (there is a northern one as well) in addition to a swim beach and picnic area.

There are several hiking and mountain biking opportunities around camp. At Loop B, you'll find the Osprey Trail (Trail 58). This 2.2-mile path has two loops and a track that leads to the water. It is named after the raptors that are commonly seen here. East of the dam is a trailhead for the Centennial Trail, the 111-mile path that traverses the Black Hills. A shorter option includes Veteran's Point at the north end of the dam. This is a .75-mile paved and handicap-accessible trail that includes picnic tables, interpretive signs, restrooms, and fishing piers.

Field Notes

This is a busy place during the summer, on the water and off. If you like to join the action, you'll enjoy this hoppin' camp. If you're looking for calmer waters, check out one of the smaller lakes such as Dalton Lake or Roubaix Lake.

Directions

From Rapid City, take HWY 44 west for 17 miles. Turn left onto HWY 385 and drive south for nearly 3 miles. Turn right onto the paved access road and follow the signs for a couple more miles to reach the recreation area.

If driving from Hill City, follow HWY 16/HWY 385 north for almost 14 miles to the turnoff on the left. Follow the paved road to the campground.

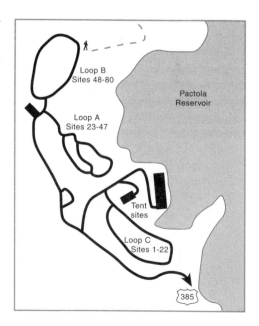

12 Bear Gulch Group Campground
Privacy and solitude on the south side of Pactola Reservoir

Map	Page 28
Usage	High
Sites	8 (up to 40 people)
Cost	$85
Camp Facilities	Fire rings, picnic tables, water, pit toilets
Spur Length	Long—up to 45 feet
Managing Agency	USDA Forest Service—Black Hills National Forest
Reservations	Accepted—check www.recreation.gov or call (877) 444-6777
Season	Open late May to early September
Elevation	4,600 feet
GPS Coordinates	N44° 4.46' W103° 31.52'

The Camp

Bear Gulch is an exclusive group camp that can accommodate up to 40 people. It offers plenty of privacy as the narrow and winding access road is gated with a lock. Only the camping group and managing agency can drive to the camp so you get no traffic other than your own.

Bear Gulch Campground

The campground is located where the mouth of Bear Gulch opens to a small cove on Pactola Reservoir. If the reservoir is at a normal or above average level, you'll enjoy waterside campsites along the shoreline. If water levels are down, the cove may be a bog, but the camp would still serve as a worthwhile place to spend a few nights. With an abundance of pine trees and steep hills, your site will be in the shadows for much of the day.

The campground consists of a main parking area where you'll find enough room to park a few trailers. Most of the designated sites are best suited for tents as they are scattered along the grassy shoreline.

This is a popular site, so reservations fill the calendar several months before the camping season even starts. However, late-comers can sometimes claim weekday nights on Tuesday, Wednesday, and Thursday. Once you have your reservation, you can get a key to the gate from the host at nearby Pactola Campground.

Field Notes
I spent an afternoon here on the shoreline with my family and it was one of the best moments during the research of this book. Calm waters, a warm sun, and the silence of the woods made me wish I was spending the night.

Directions
If coming from Rapid City, take HWY 44 west for 17 miles. Turn left onto HWY 385 and drive south for 5.1 miles. Turn right onto FR 258. Drive to a fork and then bear left onto FR 251. Follow this curvy road for 3.5 miles to a fork. Bear right onto FR 253 and follow this narrow lane for 2.9 miles to the campground.

If driving from Hill City, head north on HWY 16/HWY 385 north for 11.5 miles and turn left onto FR 258. Drive to a fork and then bear left onto FR 251. Follow this curvy road for 3.5 miles to a fork. Bear right onto FR 253 and follow this narrow lane for 2.9 miles to the campground.

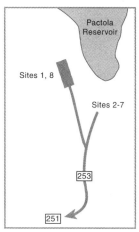

Castle Peak Campground
Primitive mountain camping away from it all

Map	Page 28
Usage	Low
Sites	9
Cost	None
Camp Facilities	Fire rings, picnic tables, pit toilets
Spur Length	Long—up to 45 feet
Managing Agency	USDA Forest Service—Black Hills National Forest
Reservations	Not accepted—first come, first served
Season	Open all year
Elevation	5,300 feet
GPS Coordinates	N44° 4.8' W103° 43.62'

The Camp
Though this is likely the most difficult camp to reach in the Black Hills, it also makes a scenic and fun drive. If you're accustomed to camping in the Rocky Mountains, the roads that bring you here will be nothing too out of the ordinary. But for those casual campers who are used to staying in private campgrounds along a highway, Castle Peak Campground will feel

Castle Peak Campground

like true wilderness. The roads are rough, with ruts, mud, and—on the western approach—some large rocks. You'll want to drive something with decent ground clearance, such as a pickup truck or SUV. The roads are also narrow with one-lane stretches, so only the smallest of trailers are usually brought here. Tents and pickup campers work best.

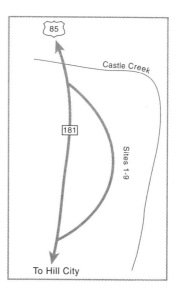

The camp shares its name with a 6,358-foot summit that stands about a half mile to the northeast—but this isn't a mount that towers over the campground and steals your attention. Rather, it's the rugged canyon terrain and Castle Creek, which runs through it, that make this such an appealing place to spend the night. The waterfront campsites are evenly spaced along an arced road in a shady stand of spruce. The picnic tables are lined along the creek, and a few are located just feet from the stream bank. On the opposing side of the camp to the west, there is a large scree slope spotted with ponderosa pine.

For its remoteness, Castle Peak gets fairly good visitation, though many of these visitors are just passing through on a day trip. Still, you won't have to fight over a site, at least outside of hunting season. If you do a little poking around the area, you can find evidence of the Black Hills' mining history. Cabin ruins and old equipment still remain around the nearby mines.

Field Notes

The water pump no longer works and there is no garbage collection, so you'll have to pack in your own water and pack out your trash.

Directions

There are two approaches to this camp: from the east and from the west. If you're wondering about road conditions, especially during the off-season or early and late in the regular season, the Forest Service can often tell you which route is in the best condition.

For an eastern approach from Hill City, take paved Deerfield Road (FR 17/CR 308) westward for 5.5 miles. Turn north onto Mystic Road (FR 231) and drive 7.2 miles. Turn left onto FR 181 and drive 8 miles along a rough and narrow dirt lane.

For a western approach from Spearfish, take HWY 14A (Spearfish Canyon Scenic Byway) southward for 18.5 miles to HWY 85 at Cheyenne Crossing. From this junction, turn left and drive east for just over 4 miles to reach paved FR 17. (You can reach this same point from Lead by taking HWY 85 southward for 3.5 miles). Now drive south for 15 miles to Rochford. Turn right and drive west on FR 231 for just .7 mile. Turn left here onto CR 306 and drive 2.8 miles. Turn left onto a dirt spur and stay right at the first unsigned fork. Now follow this rocky and rutted track, FR 181, for another 3 miles to reach the camp. Take note that these directions from the west may vary slightly from what you encounter. During the researching of this book, this area was being logged. There were no road signs and it appeared that additional roads were being constructed.

Deerfield Lake

Deerfield Lake is a 414-acre reservoir located in the center of South Dakota's Black Hills National Forest. Deerfield Dam, located on the lake's northeastern end, was constructed by several organizations including the Farm Security Administration, the Civilian Conservation Corps (CCC), and the Civilian Public Service Camp. (Incredibly, I discovered during the research of this book that my wife's grandfather was one of 500 Mennonites who helped build the structure during World War II.) After five years of work, the Bureau of Reclamation finished the project in 1947. The Bureau is still the managing agency of the dam.

The lake offers 7.5 miles of shoreline and two boat ramps that are conveniently located at two of the area's three campgrounds. The lake has a 5mph speed limit as well as a no-wake restriction. Anglers will find splake, rock bass, and both rainbow and brown trout swimming these waters. The lake is filled and drained by Castle Creek, which is itself a fishery.

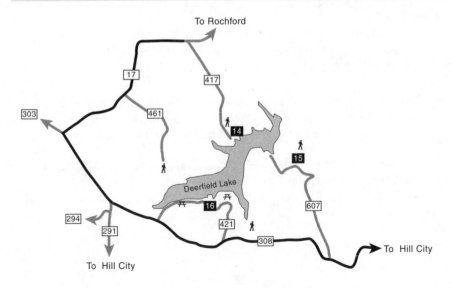

14 Custer Trail Campground
Boater's camp on the northern shoreline of Deerfield Lake

Map	Page 28, 58
Usage	Low
Sites	14
Cost	$11-$13
Camp Facilities	Fire rings, grills, picnic tables, water, pit toilets, trash containers
Spur Length	Long—up to 40 feet
Managing Agency	USDA Forest Service—Black Hills National Forest
Reservations	Not accepted—first come, first served
Season	Open late May to early September
Elevation	5,925 feet
GPS Coordinates	N44° 1.51' W103° 47.89'

The Camp

Custer Trail—named after the on-site trailhead—is a utilitarian camp that puts function over beauty, though that's not to say that overlooking the northern shoreline of Deerfield Lake isn't scenic. Still, chances are that if you find yourself camping here, you're either a boater or a camper who couldn't find a site in one of the other nearby camps.

Custer Trail Campground

The campground is best described as a gravel parking lot with a boat ramp and trailhead. There are eight primitive RV sites—parking spaces really—that comprise the lower lot. These have no trees, no space or privacy, and just a few picnic tables among all of them. The upper lot provides parking for six walk-in tent sites situated on a wooded hill of ponderosa pine. These sites each have a fire ring, grill, and some shade.

The recreation site also includes designated parking for the Custer Trail Trailhead. This serves as the western end of the Lake Loop Trail (Trail 40L), an 11-mile path that encircles the lake and climbs through the forested hills to the south. There is also boat trailer parking. If you're boating, remember that Deerfield Lake has a 5mph speed limit and creating a wake is prohibited.

Field Notes
The Forest Service states that there are 16 sites here. I counted 14. Either way, you'll likely have your choice out of all of them.

Directions
From Hill City, take paved Deerfield Road (FR 17/CR 308) westward for 17.7 miles to a fork. Stay right on FR 17 (signed as CR 306) and drive 2.5 miles to a turnoff for FR 417. Take this road 1.4 miles to reach the camp and reservoir.

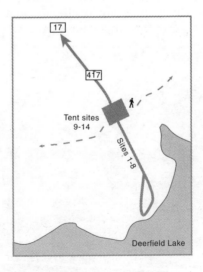

15 Dutchman Campground
Forested camping on the south side of Deerfield Lake

Map	Page 28, 58
Usage	High
Sites	45
Cost	$15 ($30 for double sites)
Camp Facilities	Fire rings, picnic tables, water, pit toilets, trash containers
Spur Length	Long—up to 50 feet
Managing Agency	USDA Forest Service—Black Hills National Forest; a host is on site
Reservations	Accepted—check www.recreation.gov or call (877) 444-6777
Season	Open late May to early September
Elevation	6,060 feet
GPS Coordinates	N44° 1.3' W103° 46.88'

The Camp
Dutchman Campground is the primary recreation site at Deerfield Lake. It's the lake's largest campground and also has the main boat ramp. With paved access most of the way, you'll find it easy to reach, but remote enough to feel like you're getting away.

Dutchman Campground

The campground consists of three separate loops with an assortment of single, double, and handicap-accessible sites. The first loop holds ten sites and is closest to the main road that leads down to the lake and boat ramp. Tucked further back into the forest are two more loops. The second and largest contains sites 11-31 while the smaller loop has sites 32-45. Campsites on the outside of these loops are spacious, but the interior sites can feel tight on busy weekends. Although there are nearly four dozen sites in all, the isolated loops, mature trees, rolling terrain, and a tall understory of grass and young pines help create separation between campers.

Since the campground is hidden in the forest, you won't have lake views. To reach the water, there is a gravel road that descends a half mile and nearly 200 vertical feet to a picnic area and boat ramp. This is a scenic place to spend some time, but be aware that a day use fee is required.

If you want to explore the area by trail, you'll find trailhead markers in camp for the 11-mile Lake Loop Trail (Trail 40L) as well as the Dutchman Loop Trail (Trail 47), a 1.7-mile path that takes you around the campground. There are also five other trailheads near the lake.

Field Notes

This camp was renovated in 2008 and includes some new facilities and signage. With a shadowy forest, lake breezes, and a high elevation, this camp is a good choice for those hot summer days.

Directions

From Hill City, take paved Deerfield Road (FR 17/CR 308) westward for 13.5 miles. Turn right on onto FR 607 and drive another 1.4 miles.

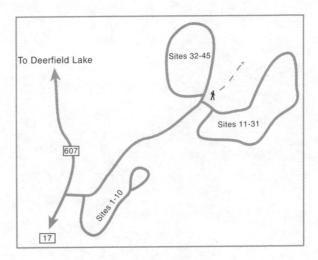

16 Whitetail Campground
Hilltop camping above Deerfield Lake

Map	Page 28, 58
Usage	High
Sites	17
Cost	$17 (no charge in off season)
Camp Facilities	Fire rings, picnic tables, water, pit toilets, trash containers
Spur Length	Long—up to 50 feet
Managing Agency	USDA Forest Service—Black Hills National Forest; a host is on site
Reservations	Accepted—check www.recreation.gov or call (877) 444-6777
Season	Open late May until snow closure
Elevation	6,000 feet
GPS Coordinates	N44° 0.75' W103° 48.18'

The Camp

Whitetail Campground is located atop a wooded hill south of Deerfield Lake. Of the three camps surrounding this reservoir, this is the medium sized one. Though it has no boat ramp or road access to the lake like the other two, it does offer sites that have a view over the water.

Whitetail Campground

The campground is divided into two loops by the gravel road that serves this campground and two nearby picnic areas. The higher loop has ten sites that are close together. The lower, northern loop includes the remaining seven sites with slightly more room. Some of these also include a view of the water and hiking access to the shoreline. Although ponderosa pines stand over both loops to provide shade, they've been thinned here so they don't provide much privacy nor do they serve as a wind break.

There are 30 miles of recreation trails (some sources show 37 miles) that traverse this area of the Black Hills. This includes the Deerfield Trail (Trail 40) which runs from the lake eastward toward Pactola Reservoir, and the Lake Loop Trail (Trail 40L). Both of these are open to foot, hoof, and bike traffic and the campground itself is popular with mountain bikers who take advantage of these trails.

Field Notes
Since many nearby campgrounds close after Labor Day, this campground sees steady use through September and October. These are great months to be here—you'll enjoy milder temperatures and less traffic.

Directions
From Hill City, take paved Deerfield Road (FR 17/CR 308) westward for 15 miles. Turn right on Whitetail Loop (FR 421) and drive just shy of another mile.

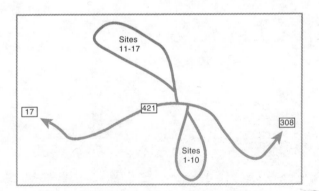

Ditch Creek Campground

17

A distant camp in the central Black Hills

Map	Page 28
Usage	Low
Sites	13
Cost	$17 (no fee during the off season)
Camp Facilities	Fire rings, picnic tables, water, pit toilets
Spur Length	Long—up to 40 feet
Managing Agency	USDA Forest Service—Black Hills National Forest
Reservations	Not accepted—first come, first served
Season	Open all year
Elevation	6,250 feet
GPS Coordinates	N43° 57.63' W103° 50.48'

The Camp

Ditch Creek is a great alternative to the busy campgrounds found at nearby Deerfield Reservoir. It's also a favorite place for ATV riders who take advantage of this area's wide network of backroads. The country here is more rugged than other nearby camps, and you'll enjoy views of conifer-covered hills with vertical rock cliffs.

Ditch Creek Campground

The camp's main loop has nine spurs in a grassy park. These are level sites that have no privacy or shade, but parking is easy. For a more timbered campsite, either choose one on the west side of the loop, or head south on the campground road to reach sites 11, 12, and 13, which are tucked into the tall spruce forest.

Ditch Creek runs along the west side of the camp and fills some nearby beaver ponds. The stream is fishable, but you can also head north for 4 miles to Deerfield Reservoir. Hiking and biking trails are also available at the reservoir.

Field Notes

You are either going to find solitude at this camp or the buzz of motors—it all depends on your neighbors. On one visit, this camp felt like a lonely nook in the wilderness. On another, there were groups of ATV riders who motored about the roads. Either way, the local campers who come to Ditch Creek often just want to get away from the more populated areas of the Hills.

Directions

To reach the camp from Hill City, take paved Deerfield Road (FR 17/CR 308) westward for 16.7 miles to FR 291. Turn south and follow this gravel road for 4.3 miles to the camp.

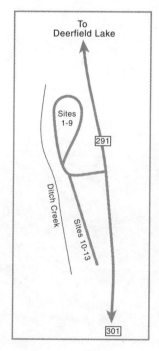

18 Beaver Creek Campground
Remote camping on the state line

Map	Page 28
Usage	Low
Sites	8
Cost	$10 (no fee during the off season)
Camp Facilities	Fire rings, picnic tables, water, pit toilets
Spur Length	Long—up to 45 feet
Managing Agency	USDA Forest Service—Black Hills National Forest
Reservations	Not accepted—first come, first served
Season	Open all year
Elevation	6,500 feet
GPS Coordinates	N44° 4.49' W104° 3.01'

The Camp
Beaver Creek Campground is located on the South Dakota-Wyoming border. At 6,500 feet, this is one of the highest campgrounds in South Dakota, and also one of the wettest ones in the Black Hills. The increased elevation and precipitation is evident in the dense surrounding forest, which is comprised of spruce, pine, and aspen.

Beaver Creek Campground

The roomy sites are mostly in the open, situated around a grassy park that is lined with large rocks that define parking spots. The flat area is perfect for tent camping, or daytime activities such as yard sports. Sites 3-6 are ideal for groups that need multiple sites that are together. These four are situated in the middle of the camp, in the grassy area, and three of them are on a single large pullout. You'll likely get the site you want and need, as camping use is very light. I've never actually seen anyone camping here, though a few outdated permits on the site posts prove that it does receive at least occasional use.

Beaver Creek runs along the side of the camp and a small footbridge spans the stream. Two miles east of the camp, you'll find a trailhead for the Beaver Creek Ski Area, which has six cross-country ski trails of nearly 13 miles that cut through the forest near the campground. One of these is a groomed snowmobile trail.

Field Notes

Unless it's been logged since this writing, you'll find tremendous timber damage along the road to the east and northeast. This blowdown was the result of a tornado that ripped through here in June, 2008. The storm left an impressive swath of flattened spruce and snapped trunks.

Directions

There are many ways to reach this distant campground. Most of these use long, gravel roads that will have you reaching for a national forest map. For a mostly paved route from Spearfish, take HWY 14A (Spearfish Canyon Scenic Byway) southward for 18.5 miles to HWY 85 at Cheyenne Crossing. From this junction, turn right, and drive west 25.5 miles to Mallo Camp Road, just past the intersection for HWY 585 at Four Corners. (You can also reach this point from Newcastle, Wyoming by driving north on HWY 85 for 18 miles.) Head east on Mallow Camp Road (CR 811/FR 111) for 6 miles to reach the camp.

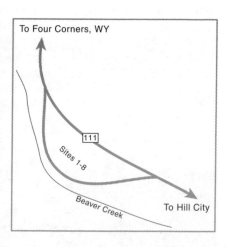

To reach the camp from Hill City, take paved FR 17 (Deerfield Road) westward for 17.7 miles to a fork. Stay straight by taking the left fork and drive 12 miles on FR 110/CR 303. When you reach FR 109, turn left and drive 3.2 miles. Turn right onto FR 111 and head west for the last 1.7 miles.

19 Redbank Springs Campground
Remote ATV encampment on the western edge of the Black Hills

Map	Page 28
Usage	Low
Sites	4
Cost	$10 (no fee during the off season)
Camp Facilities	Fire rings, picnic tables, pit toilets
Spur Length	Long—up to 40 feet
Managing Agency	USDA Forest Service—Black Hills National Forest
Reservations	Not accepted—first come, first served
Season	Open all year
Elevation	6,600 feet
GPS Coordinates	N43° 59.43' W103° 58.87'

The Camp

Redbank Springs Campground is tucked away in a forgotten area of the Black Hills. Located just a few miles from the Wyoming border, and many more miles from the area's popular attractions, this isn't a place you just come across on your way to some other destination.

Looking east from Redbank Springs Campground

The camp sits at the end of a 1-mile dead-end lane, so there is no passing traffic. The sites overlook a sprawling mountain park that is bound by aspen stands and pine-covered hills. Redbank Spring, a small pond, is close to the campground's entrance.

The camp itself is tiny, but the sites—especially sites 1 and 2—are very spacious. A couple of them have gravel spurs, but the others are overgrown with grass and show little use. A mixed forest of conifers and deciduous trees fill in the spaces, provide shade, and make this a pretty camp.

While there are no developed recreation sites in the surrounding vicinity, this is a good camp for those like to view wildlife, hike off-trail, hunt, or ride ATVs along the lonely backroads of the western Black Hills National Forest. The camp has an ATV trailer parking area between the first two sites. If you do have ATVs, you'll find miles of rugged tracks west and south of the campground that make for great riding.

Field Notes

For this camp my field notes simply stated, "Truly away from it all." Worth noting is that the Forest Service lists this camp as open all year. However, a sign at the campground declares the area to be closed from December 15th to May 15th.

Directions

To reach this camp from Hill City, take paved Deerfield Road (FR 17/CR 308) westward for 16.7 miles to FR 291. Turn south and follow this road for only a tenth of a mile before turning right onto FR 294. Now follow this winding, gravel lane for 4.3 miles to a junction. Stay on FR 294 by turning left and drive another 9 miles to a campground sign. Turn right onto the access road and drive north for less than a mile.

There are many other ways to get to this campground, especially if you are coming from Custer or Wyoming. A Black Hills National Forest map will help determine your best route.

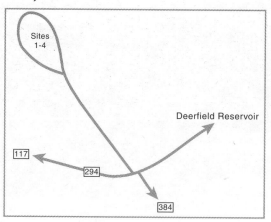

Moon Campground
A long, long way from everywhere

Map	Page 28
Usage	Low
Sites	3
Cost	None
Camp Facilities	Fire rings, picnic tables, pit toilets
Spur Length	Medium—up to 35 feet
Managing Agency	USDA Forest Service—Black Hills National Forest
Reservations	Not accepted—first come, first served
Season	Open all year
Elevation	6,400 feet
GPS Coordinates	N43° 56.78' W104° 0.5'

The Camp

Moon Campground is about as far away from the region's tourist attractions as you can get. You don't come here if you want to see Mount Rushmore; you come here to escape the crowds, explore the rugged western hills of South Dakota, and maybe hunt deer in the fall.

Moon Campground

The camp is found in tall evergreens just 2.3 miles from the Wyoming–South Dakota state line. Old log cabins next to the camp are privately-owned remnants of an old ghost town named Moon. Next to them, you'll find a tiny, shaded loop with three grassy sites that see little use. Remember to pack in your own water and pack out your trash—this is primitive camping by Black Hills standards.

So what is there to do here? You'll have to find your own outdoor activities as there are no nearby developed trails or fishing areas. However, if you love driving the lonely backroads of the Black Hills, this is your camp. There are many miles of gravel lanes and rough tracks in this part of the national forest.

Field Notes

This is one of the highest campgrounds in South Dakota and is more than twice as high as those camps around the fringe of the Black Hills. As a result, you can expect your summer nights and mornings to be a little crisper. Snow also comes easier here.

Directions

To reach this remote camp from Hill City, take paved Deerfield Road (FR 17/CR 308) westward for 16.7 miles to FR 291. Turn south and follow this gravel road for nearly 8 miles to a four-way intersection. Turn right on Sixmile Road (FR 301) and drive west for 10 miles to the end of this road. Turn left onto FR 117 and watch for the campground entrance on your right.

To reach the camp from Custer, drive west on HWY 16 for 27.5 miles. Turn north on FR 117 and drive north for 15 miles.

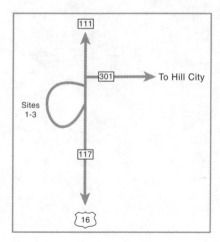

21 Sheridan North Cove Group Campground
Large group sites at Sheridan Reservoir

Map	Page 28
Usage	High
Sites	5
Cost	$50-$150
Camp Facilities	Fire rings, grills, picnic tables, water, pit toilets, trash containers, boat ramp, amphitheater
Spur Length	Not applicable; parking lots instead of spurs
Managing Agency	USDA Forest Service—Black Hills National Forest; a host is on site
Reservations	Accepted—check www.recreation.gov or call (877) 444-6777
Season	Open late May to early September
Elevation	4,650 feet
GPS Coordinates	N43° 58.94' W103° 28.26'

The Camp
North Cove is an impressive group campground near the northern shoreline of Sheridan Lake. It has easy access to a boat ramp and swim beach. A nearby marina offers a restaurant, store, fuel, boat rentals, fishing supplies, slip rentals, and boat storage.

Sheridan North Cove Group Campground

There are five group sites that can accommodate up to 270 people. The first of these is the Susie Squirrel (SS1) site. This is a timbered and shady area intended for 55 people. It is completely separated from the other four sites and has its own parking lot that accommodates up to 15 cars. The second site, Ranger Rick (RR1), is the largest and holds up to 100 people. The parking lot has 25 parking spaces, but there is also an adjacent lot with an additional 25 spots.

The remaining three loops share a common parking area that holds up to sixty cars. They include Davey Deer (DD1), Billie Beaver (BB1), and Ollie Otter (OO1). They hold 30 people, 25 people, and 60 people, respectively. Davey Dear is a timbered site while the others have a grassy area that is surrounded by pines.

Field Notes

If you've got a large group coming (close to the site's capacity), you'll want to be sure to carpool. There is one overflow parking lot, but it is shared among all of the sites.

Directions

From Hill City, drive north on HWY 385 for 6.5 miles and turn right on Sheridan Lake Road (HWY 228). Drive a quarter mile east and then bear right at a fork and follow the signs to the campground.

If driving from Rapid City, follow Sheridan Lake Road (CR 228) west for 16.7 miles. Just before reaching HWY 385, turn left and follow the signs to the campground.

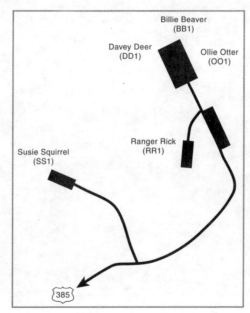

22 Sheridan Lake Southside Campground
Sprawling campground along a popular reservoir

Map	Page 28
Usage	High
Sites	129
Cost	$21 ($10 during the off season)
Camp Facilities	Fire rings, picnic tables, water, pit toilets, trash containers, boat ramp
Spur Length	Long—up to 60 feet
Managing Agency	USDA Forest Service—Black Hills National Forest; multiple hosts are on site
Reservations	Accepted—check www.recreation.gov or call (877) 444-6777
Season	Open all year
Elevation	4,750 feet
GPS Coordinates	N43° 58.0' W103° 28.69'

The Camp
Like nearby Pactola Reservoir, Sheridan Lake receives its name from a gold-rush town that was flooded when the reservoir was finished by the Civilian Conservation Corps (CCC) in 1940. The lake covers 375 acres and has 7.5 miles of shoreline. Today, it's a recreational hotspot for boating, fishing, swimming, camping, and picnicking.

Sheridan Lake Southside Campground

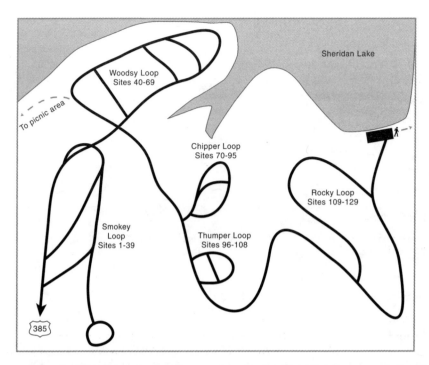

The timbered gentle knolls on the south side of the reservoir hold Sheridan Lake Southside, the largest campground in the Black Hills National Forest. This is a complex recreation site that has a dizzying layout of loops, connector roads, and spurs. All roads are paved and it's an easy camp to drive around, though you may need to make a few passes to figure out where you are going.

After passing a picnic area and climbing a grade from the nearby highway, you'll reach the campground entrance where you'll find signs for various loops. The first of these is the Smokey Loop, which has 39 campsites. Further north is the Woodsy Loop (actually several interconnected loops) with sites 40-69. These include prime spots with lakeside views and access to the shoreline. The remaining sites, 70-129, are found on the Chipper, Thumper, and Rocky Loops, all of which are reached by following the road that leads to the boat ramp, trailhead, and swim beach. Some spots in the Rocky Loop (sites 109-129) have views of the lake while the other two loops are located higher in the forest.

You'll find parking spurs to be long, level and accommodating for big rigs. Privacy between campers mostly depends on how busy and crowded the campground is. When this place nears capacity, it's bustling! Make your visit in the off season when only the Woodsy Loop is open, and you'll have plenty of space and solitude.

If you're coming to the lake to fish, you'll find perch, trout, northern pike, and bass. There are two boat ramps—the one here at the campground and another on the northern shoreline along with a marina, store, and large swim beach. You'll also find a few fishing piers around the lake.

Next to the boat ramp is Calumet Trailhead, which accesses the Centennial Trail (Trail 89) and Flume Trail (50). The Centennial Trail is a 111-mile path that crosses the Black Hills from north to south. The access point here at the campground is around the trail's halfway point. The Flume Trail meanders east of the lake for 16.5 miles. This foot path is considered one of the most scenic and worthwhile trails in the national forest. You'll encounter meadows, tunnels, and interpretive signage that describes the area's gold mining history. A trail map is recommended as both trails have many junctions that tie into other trail networks.

Field Notes

This is one massive campground and you can get a good workout just by walking around the campground's loops. An evening stroll from my campsite to the boat ramp and back was a 3-mile trek. Be warned: the bats are thick here at dusk.

Directions

From Hill City, drive north on HWY 385 for 5 miles. If driving from Rapid City, follow Sheridan Lake Road (CR 228) west for 17 miles. Turn south on HWY 385 and drive 1.5 miles to the camp turnoff.

Sheridan Lake

Black Hills National Forest

SOUTHERN BLACK HILLS
CAMPGROUNDS SOUTH OF HILL CITY
INCLUDING BADLANDS NATIONAL PARK

The southern half of the Black Hills—the area south of Hill City—is truly an American playground. Up to three million people visit Mount Rushmore every year. Nearby Custer State Park draws nearly two million visitors and Badlands National Park brings in another million. Adding to these popular national treasures is Wind Cave National Park, Jewel Cave National Monument, and roughly half a million acres of public land in the surrounding Black Hills National Forest.

The reasons people come here are as varied as the attractions they visit. Thousands come to witness the annual buffalo fall roundup in Custer State Park. Some explore the primitive backcountry by saddle, guiding their horses along miles of trails. Others use their fingertips and toes to climb granite walls. Throughout the summer, but primarily in August when the Sturgis motorcycle rally is underway, bikers cruise the Hills' scenic byways. Camping families relish the many small fishing lakes, moderate hiking trails, and mild climate of the area. More still spend their days taking a helicopter tour, train ride, swimming in the world's largest indoor pool in the town of Hot Springs, or shopping the rustic storefronts in the small mountain communities. Indeed, this is an American playground.

Southern Black Hills Campgrounds

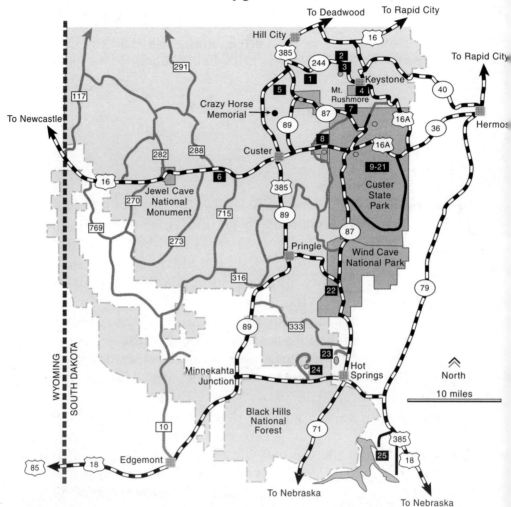

Badlands National Park

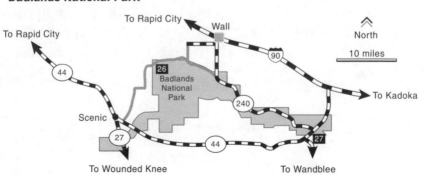

Campground Number	Campground Name	Page Number
1	Willow Creek Horse Camp	82
2	Wrinkled Rock Climber's Trailhead	84
3	Horsethief Lake Campground	86
4	Grizzly Creek Campground	89
5	Oreville Campground	91
6	Comanche Park Campground	93
7	Iron Creek Horse Camp	95
8	Bismarck Lake Campground	97
9	Sylvan Lake Campground	101
10	Center Lake Non-Profit Youth Camp	104
11	Center Lake Campground	106
12	Stockade Lake North Campground	108
13	Stockade Lake South Campground	110
14	Stockade Lake Group Camp Area	112
15	Legion Lake Campground	114
16	Shady Rest Non-Profit Youth Camp	116
17	Grace Coolidge Campground	118
18	Game Lodge Group Camping Area	120
19	Game Lodge Campground	122
20	Blue Bell Campground	124
21	French Creek Horse Camp	126
22	Elk Mountain Campground	129
23	Cold Brook Lake Campground	131
24	Cottonwood Springs Lake Campground	133
25	Angostura Recreation Area Campgrounds	136
26	Sage Creek Campground	140
27	Cedar Pass Campground	142

Willow Creek Horse Camp

Horse camping near Keystone

Map	Page 80
Usage	High
Sites	8 group sites
Cost	$24-$100 (no fee during the off season)
Camp Facilities	Fire rings, picnic tables, pit toilets, water, trash containers, hitching posts and lines, horse water tanks
Spur Length	Medium to long—between 35 and 100 feet
Managing Agency	USDA Forest Service—Black Hills National Forest
Reservations	Accepted—check www.recreation.gov or call (877) 444-6777
Season	Open all year
Elevation	5,000 feet
GPS Coordinates	N43° 53.86' W103° 32.21'

The Camp

Compared to the sprawling KOA resort with mini-golf, a waterslide, and restaurant on the other side of the highway, Willow Creek Horse Camp feels like another planet. There is no cable TV or wireless Internet here, just big trucks, bigger trailers, and passionate horse owners with their animals.

Willow Creek Horse Camp

This group camp represents horse camping at its finest. At its core is trailhead parking and a staging area. From here, the sites are lined along two roads that are separated by a hill. One lane extends into the Palmer Creek drainage and the other along Willow Creek. The greatest distance between these two roads is nearly a quarter mile. Bottom line—you won't be crammed in next to your neighbors here.

The group sites are spacious, accommodating between 4 and 16 people each. Some allow one rig (defined as one vehicle and one trailer) while others allow up to six rigs. There is a good mix of back-in spurs and pull-throughs. When making a reservation, you'll want to check the website for the site that best fits your needs as spur lengths vary. You'll find your campsite to be nicely wooded in a pine forest and includes hitching posts, lines, and a grassy flat. There are a couple of corrals, but not individual ones like at Iron Creek Horse Camp. Remember that weed-free certified hay is required in the national forest.

For riding trails, you have three options directly from the campground. The shortest is Trail 8, the 1.5-mile Willow Creek Loop. The northern part of this loop utilizes Trail 9, which ultimately heads southward into the Black Elk Wilderness. Another option is Trail 2, the Lost Cabin Trail, which works southwest to the heart of the Harney Range toward Sylvan Lake.

Field Notes

This is such a peaceful setting. When I drove into camp, I felt like I was barreling an 18-wheeler into a residential cul-de-sac. There were no revving ATVs or blaring stereos, just a restful place where folks ride horses at whatever pace suits them.

Directions

From Keystone, take HWY 16A southward to HWY 244. Then drive west on HWY 244 for 7.4 miles to the camp on the left. If driving from Hill City, take HWY 16/HWY 385 south for 3 miles. Turn left onto HWY 244 and drive east for 3.1 miles to the camp on the right.

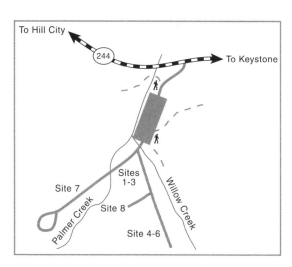

2 Wrinkled Rock Climber's Trailhead
Climber's bivy camp behind Mount Rushmore

Map	Page 80
Usage	Moderate to high
Sites	No designated sites
Cost	None
Camp Facilities	Pit toilets, trash containers
Spur Length	Not applicable—parking for cars only
Managing Agency	USDA Forest Service—Black Hills National Forest
Reservations	Not accepted—first come, first served
Season	Open all year
Elevation	5,200 feet
GPS Coordinates	N43° 53.23' W103° 28.16'

The Camp
Wrinkled Rock is a small parking area that is adjacent to the rock walls and formations on the west side of Mount Rushmore. From here, climbers can reach some outstanding routes.

Wrinkled Rock Climber's Trailhead

The site is intended to be used by climbers who just need a tent or bivy site without many other facilities or services. The Forest Service encourages campers to choose a no-impact site near your car rather than push further into the forest where you'll create more of an environmental disturbance.

The camp has a roof of towering evergreens, so finding a tent spot on a durable bed of pine needles is easy to do. You'll also find large boulders that are just the right size for sitting, cooking, or setting out your gear. There is no charge for staying here, but RVs, trailers, and generators are prohibited. Campfires are also not allowed.

Field Notes
If you're traveling light and don't need much, this is the perfect place—and you can't beat the price. Just don't forget to bring your own water.

Directions
From Keystone, take HWY 16A southward to HWY 244. Then drive west on HWY 244 for 3.2 miles to the camp on the right. If driving from Hill City, take HWY 16/HWY 385 south for 3 miles. Turn left onto HWY 244 and drive east 7.3 miles to the camp on the left.

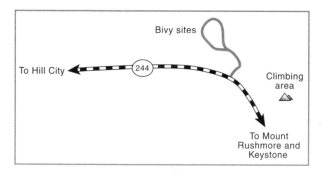

3 Horsethief Lake Campground
Crowded and gorgeous camp near Mount Rushmore

Map	Page 80
Usage	High
Sites	36
Cost	$23
Camp Facilities	Fire rings, picnic tables, water, pit toilets, trash containers
Spur Length	Short—most up to 25 feet, a few longer for RVs
Managing Agency	USDA Forest Service—Black Hills National Forest; a host is on site
Reservations	Accepted—check www.recreation.gov or call (877) 444-6777
Season	Open late May to early September
Elevation	4,960 feet
GPS Coordinates	N43° 53.72' W103° 29.05'

The Camp

Horsethief Lake Campground is the Forest Service's premiere camp in the Black Hills. If you don't already know this, you'll realize it as soon as you pull in on the paved road and see the staffed information booth instead of a self-service pay tube.

The recreation site has a lot going for it. For one, it's fewer than three miles to Mount Rushmore. Secondly, it includes a gorgeous lake surrounded by hills of ponderosa pine and granite. Third, it has a trail that wraps around the lake as well as a trailhead that accesses the Centennial Trail and Black Elk Wilderness. Last, it's located along the Peter Norbeck Scenic Byway, which means you'll find spectacular scenery no matter which way you come or go.

The camp layout is unique. The first sites—1 through 8 and 19 through 22—offer the best spacing and privacy, though it's hard to write that with a straight face. The next set, 9 through 18, are packed together along a curve. All of these can be used for tents, trailers, and RVs, but parking spur lengths greatly vary. Some will barely accommodate a single vehicle while others will park a fifth-wheel trailer. Fortunately, the reservation website gives lengths for each campsite. The next sites, 32-36, are walk-in tent sites on a small timbered rise with communal fire rings and seating benches. Campsites 23-28 are tent-only sites that are separated from the rest of the campground and found closer to the lake.

If you're looking for a quiet camping experience where cricket chirping competes with campfire crackling, you won't find it here. Some of the tent pads between sites are a mere four feet from each other—you could actually be sleeping closer to your neighbor than to some of your own campmates.

On the other hand, the camp puts you in the middle of postcard scenery in one of America's vacation hotspots. When you see tourists on the highway pull over to photograph the very lake where you are camping, you can't help but feel satisfied that you've claimed a spot here.

Naturally, reservations are recommended far in advance. However, not all sites can be reserved, so it's worth stopping by around mid-morning (especially mid-week) to see if you can score a fresh vacancy. Unfortunately, the camp is closed most of September, which is a gorgeous time to visit the Hills and this lake.

Horsethief Lake

Field Notes

There is also a private campground on HWY 87 near Sylvan Lake that has the same name, so be sure you know where you want to go before following directions on signs or in advertisements.

Directions

From Keystone, take HWY 16A southward to HWY 244. Then drive west on HWY 244 for 4.5 miles to the camp on the left. If driving from Hill City, take HWY 16/HWY 385 south for 3 miles. Turn left onto HWY 244 and drive east 6 miles to the camp on the right.

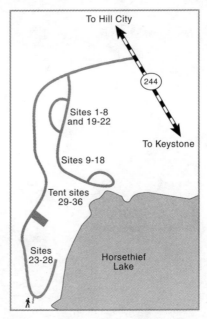

4 Grizzly Creek Campground
Tent camping along Iron Mountain Road

Map	Page 80
Usage	High
Sites	16
Cost	$19-$21
Camp Facilities	Fire rings, picnic tables, water, pit toilets, trash containers
Spur Length	Short—up to 25 feet
Managing Agency	USDA Forest Service—Black Hills National Forest; a host is on site
Reservations	Accepted—check www.recreation.gov or call (877) 444-6777
Season	Open late May to early September
Elevation	4,500 feet
GPS Coordinates	N43° 52.61' W103° 26.39'

The Camp

Grizzly Creek Campground is an excellent tent camp that's close to South Dakota's biggest attractions. Hidden behind the dense foliage of Grizzly Creek, which parallels the adjacent highway, the camp is also covered by a shadowy forest of oak and ponderosa pine. The setting feels much more remote than it is.

Grizzly Creek Campground

The cardinal rule of this campground is that only tents or single vehicle campers (like a camper van or pickup camper) are allowed. If you're towing anything, even a short motorcycle trailer, you'll have to pass on this one.

The camp has a single, tight loop and the parking spurs are short—most are just long enough to park your car. There are 20 sites, but sites 3, 4, 11, and 14 are designated as picnic use only. Set up camp next to one of these and you'll have a little more room and privacy throughout the night.

This is a popular area and if you want to stay here, you'll need to make your reservations early. Mount Rushmore is less than an air mile to the west (3.5 miles to drive there) and the town of Keystone is just a couple miles to the north. It's also located near the high-traffic junction where HWY 244, HWY 40, and HWY 16A (Iron Mountain Road) all intersect. Two of these highways, including the one in front of the campground, partially comprise the 66-mile Peter Norbeck Scenic Byway. The highlights of this byway—the pigtail bridges and rock tunnels—are found just south of the campground entrance.

Field Notes
Despite the name of the camp and creek, there are no bears here! However, you may hear the roaring of a different kind—motorcycles, and lots of them as they congregate in the Black Hills in early August.

Directions
From Keystone, take Iron Mountain Road (HWY 16A) southward for almost 2 miles to the camp on the right.

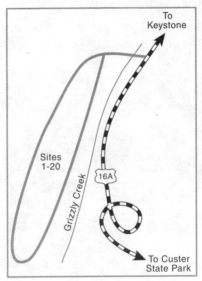

5 Oreville Campground
Central campground with easy access to popular attractions

Map	Page 80
Usage	High
Sites	26
Cost	$19
Camp Facilities	Fire rings, picnic tables, pit toilets, water, trash containers
Spur Length	Long—up to 50 feet
Managing Agency	USDA Forest Service—Black Hills National Forest; a host is on site
Reservations	Accepted—check www.recreation.gov or call (877) 444-6777
Season	Open late May to early September
Elevation	5,330 feet
GPS Coordinates	N43° 52.65' W103° 36.73'

The Camp
Oreville Campground is a beautiful camp with a manicured appearance. Tucked into a pine and aspen woodland that is flanked by interesting granite outcroppings, this is a worthwhile and scenic place to spend your camping vacation.

Oreville Campground

The campground has a paved loop road with a center lane that divides it into two sections. The front sites have little privacy and are separated from the highway by only a fence. The campsites found further back and uphill offer a lot of privacy due to a thick understory. RV campers will appreciate long parking spurs that are easy to back into and tent campers will find grassy areas that make comfortable pitching spots.

The camp is conveniently located along HWY 16 between Hill City and Custer. From this central point, you've got easy access to not only these great western communities, but also to the Black Hills' most popular destinations. The closest of these is the Needles Highway—part of the Peter Norbeck Scenic Byway—just 2 miles to the north. The Crazy Horse Memorial is fewer than five miles to the south. The George S. Mickelson Trail, a converted 109-mile railroad bed, runs along the other side of the highway. This trail is open to bikers, hikers, and horseback riders.

Field Notes

This campground may seem like an easy choice, but the adjacent highway is likely to be a deciding factor. On one hand, it's great to spend your days out touring the Black Hills and know that your camp is easy to get to, especially if it's late. The downside is that it's a very busy road, and you'll hear and see heavy traffic throughout the day and even into the night. If this is bothersome, you may want to get a little further off the beaten path.

Directions

From Hill City, drive south on HWY 16/HWY 385 for 4.7 miles. If driving from Custer, drive north on this same highway for 8 miles.

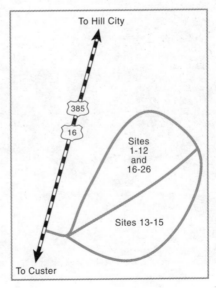

6 Comanche Park Campground
Quiet camp away from the crowds

Map	Page 80
Usage	Low
Sites	34
Cost	$15 (no fee during the off season)
Camp Facilities	Fire rings, picnic tables, water, pit toilets, trash containers
Spur Length	Long—up to 45 feet
Managing Agency	USDA Forest Service—Black Hills National Forest; a host is on site
Reservations	Accepted—check www.recreation.gov or call (877) 444-6777
Season	Open all year
Elevation	5,500 feet
GPS Coordinates	N43° 44.12' W103° 42.80'

The Camp

Comanche Park Campground—named after Comanche, a mustang in General Custer's Cavalry—isn't a very busy camp, and the people who stay here like it that way. Although it is close to Jewel Cave National Monument and Custer State Park, it's too far west for most campers, leaving plenty of solitude for those who want it.

Comanche Park Campground

Located directly off HWY 16 and replete with long parking spurs, the campground can fit those big RVs and trailers. The first five sites near the entrance are crammed together and suitable for tent use. These five are open during the off-season. Further back in a grassy ponderosa pine forest, you'll find two loops with almost three dozen more spurs and pull-throughs—plenty of capacity here considering only about a third of these are occupied on any given summer weekend.

Spacing between campers is adequate, especially if you choose a site on the outside of the loop which leaves you a huge backyard in which to tromp around or play. Nights are pleasant and calm here. Only the distant rumble of a passing vehicle on the highway, and an occasional noise from residential properties to the south, break the evening silence.

Field Notes

I've spent more nights here than any other campground in the Black Hills. If you're more interested in the undeveloped parts of the Black Hills rather than the tourist hotspots, this might be a good location for you. Drive west of the camp for about a mile to find FR 287. This is your gateway to many miles of lonely backroads that traverse beautiful country. For one worthwhile trip, grab a forest map and follow the roads north to the Bear Mountain Lookout.

Directions

From Custer, take HWY 16A west for 6 miles. The campground is on the south side of the highway.

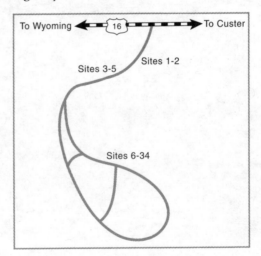

7 Iron Creek Horse Camp
Horse campground near the Needles Highway

Map	Page 80, 100
Usage	High
Sites	9
Cost	$22
Camp Facilities	Fire rings, picnic tables, pit toilets, trash containers, corrals, horse water tanks
Spur Length	Long—up to 50 feet
Managing Agency	USDA Forest Service—Black Hills National Forest
Reservations	Accepted—check www.recreation.gov or call (877) 444-6777
Season	Open late May to early September
Elevation	5,070 feet
GPS Coordinates	N43° 49.59' W103° 28.35'

The Camp

Iron Creek Horse Camp is located just a tenth of a mile north of Custer State Park in the Norbeck Wildlife Preserve. Designated by Congress in 1920, the preserve's 34,255 acres, the bulk of which are located within the Black Hills National Forest, were set aside for the protection and management of game animals and birds.

Iron Creek Horse Camp

Many consider this area of the preserve to be the Hills' true backcountry, free of roads and development and encompassing primitive areas such as the Black Elk Wilderness. Since travel through the undeveloped portions of the preserve is done on trails open to foot and hoof traffic, it's quite ideal (and progressive) to combine a trailhead with a camp designed for horseback-riding campers. The Forest Service offers two such camps: this one here along Iron Creek and also Willow Creek Horse Camp at the north end of the preserve.

The campground is arranged around a single loop that is bisected by the brushy Iron Creek drainage. While the camp itself is open, it's surrounded by pines and rock outcroppings. Campsites are grouped in tight pairs on the outside of the loop. There are no back-in parking spurs here, you just pull off parallel to the road with your truck and horse trailer and call it done. Parking areas are about fifty feet long—if you're over that, you'll fit better at Willow Creek Horse Camp.

A metal corral at each site holds two or three horses. Though there is no water here for campers, there is a water tank at each end of the camp for your animals. Also, remember that certified weed-free hay is required on the national forest.

From within the campground, you have direct access to the Norbeck Trail, which heads westward toward the Needles area of the Harney Range. In addition, there is a number of other nearby trailheads that you can use to access the Centennial Trail, Iron Mountain Trail, Iron Creek Trail, Grizzly Bear Creek Trail, and Centennial Bypass Trail.

Field Notes
This is a fantastic facility for anyone who wants to spend a few days camping and riding their horses in the mountains.

Directions
From Custer, drive east on HWY 16A for 7.3 miles. Turn left on HWY 87 (Needles Highway) and follow it north and west for 5.6 miles. Turn right onto Remington Camp Road and drive a short distance before turning left onto Iron Camp Road. Follow this lane a short distance to the campground. Due to the tunnels and narrow, curvy road, access from the west side of the Needles Highway is not recommended.

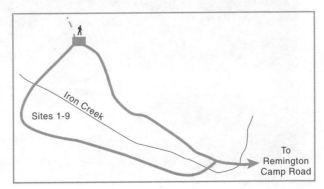

8 Bismarck Lake Campground
A perfect lakeside getaway

Map	Page 80, 100
Usage	High
Sites	23
Cost	$19 (no fee during the off season)
Camp Facilities	Fire rings, picnic tables, water, pit toilets, trash containers, boat ramp
Spur Length	Long—up to 45 feet
Managing Agency	USDA Forest Service—Black Hills National Forest; a host is on site
Reservations	Accepted—check www.recreation.gov or call (877) 444-6777
Season	Open all year
Elevation	5,250 feet
GPS Coordinates	N43° 46.50' W103° 30.77'

The Camp
Just minutes east of the conveniences in Custer (the town), and right on the boundary of Custer State Park, Bismarck Lake Campground—sometimes spelled Bismark Lake—has an ideal location. It's centrally located for day trips to Mount Rushmore, Sylvan Lake, Wind Cave National Park, Jewel Cave National Monument, and of course, Custer State Park. But

Bismark Lake

you may not even want to leave the camp. Perched above a beautiful lake and engulfed in an attractive, diverse forest, this campground serves as a destination as much as it does a base camp.

The campground is just far enough off the highway that you won't see traffic passing by, as you can in some of the other nearby camps. This is not a flat campground, and in fact, it has two levels. The upper level includes a mix of parking spurs and pull-throughs along two loops. These are long and level pads that are best suited for big rigs or multiple vehicles, but they also have tent platforms. The lower road—the one that leads to the lake—contains the remaining sites. These spurs are shorter and tighter and work well for tents or truck campers. The lower sites remain open throughout the off season.

Several foot paths lead down to the lake and you'll also find a short interpretive trail with boardwalks along the shoreline. Boats and watercrafts are allowed on the lake, but only if they are manually powered or have electric motors.

The campground is a cheaper alternative than staying inside Custer State Park where fees are higher. However, this comes at the cost of a few luxuries—you won't have showers and the sites do not have electricity. As with other nearby campgrounds, you'll want to make reservations if you're planning a trip during the busy season as the camp is often full.

Field Notes

Pretty forest and terrain—check. Scenic lake—check. Close to other attractions—check. This camp has all the right requisites for your camping trip.

Directions

From Custer, take HWY 16A east for 4 miles to the turnoff on the left side of the road.

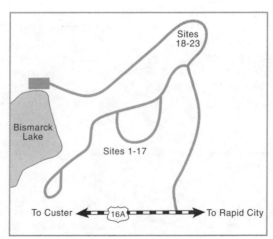

Custer State Park

Few state parks in America are as popular or large as Custer State Park, a rectangular shaped, 71,000-acre wildlife refuge on the southeast side of the Black Hills. Custer's appeal is difficult to characterize because it's so well known for many different things. There are rolling hills with roaming bison, spectacular drives over twisting bridges and through rock tunnels, shadowy pine forests, towering rock spires, placid lakes, outstanding facilities, and more than a fair share of recreational opportunities.

For motorized exploration, the park includes two scenic byways as well as a wildlife loop. The first, the Needles Highway (HWY 87), was completed in 1922 and travels 14 winding miles through the Harney Range—the park's highlands of rock and forest. This is quite possibly the most spectacular route in the region. Towering, pointed granite formations called the Needles and Cathedral Spires will have you reaching for your camera. The road passes through three narrow tunnels, which fascinate most drivers and intimidate some. Be aware of the physical dimensions of your vehicle, especially large campers. The shortest tunnel is just 10′ 4″ high. The narrowest is only 9 feet wide.

The second drive is the 17-mile Iron Mountain Road (HWY 16A). This connects HWY 36 on the eastern side of Custer State Park to Mount Rushmore and the town of Keystone to the north. This road is best known for its spiraling pigtail-shaped bridges and rock tunnels that frame Mount Rushmore in the distance—the views through the tunnels will turn you into a patriot if you're not already one. Again, take note of the tunnels' dimensions, which only measure 12′ wide and 9′ 7″ high.

The Wildlife Loop Road in the southern half of the park is quite different from the northern scenic byways. This 18-mile route passes through rolling grasslands where you'll find wildlife such as bison and antelope. You may also spot coyotes, elk, and even a few begging burros. Donkeys were originally brought here in the 1920s as pack animals, but these later generations have since become roamers.

Another scenic drive that you'll discover is the Peter Norbeck Scenic Byway. This is a 70-mile route that creates a loop through the Black Hills National Forest and Custer State Park. In the park, it incorporates both Iron Mountain Road and the Needles Highway. In the national forest, it follows HWY 244 west to east between HWY 16 and Keystone.

There are many options for non-motorized exploration. If you travel vertically, you'll find many routes up the granite walls and spires in the park. There are local guiding services that can help. For cross-country travel, there are miles of backcountry trails that are open to hikers, horses, and mountain bikers. Paddlers will find many calm lakes in which to row, and motorized boaters will also find suitable waters. Anglers have a good selection of ponds, lakes, and streams where lines can be cast for trout, perch, northern pike, and others.

Facilities in the park are top rate. The park has numerous lodges where you'll find whatever you might need. Most lodges include a general store, restaurant, lounge, watercraft and bike rentals, lodging, and Internet access. The park's campgrounds remove the primitive aspects of camping. You'll find electric hookups, showers, restrooms, and even a couple of laundromats. Naturalist programs are presented at many of the camps each evening.

Custer State Park

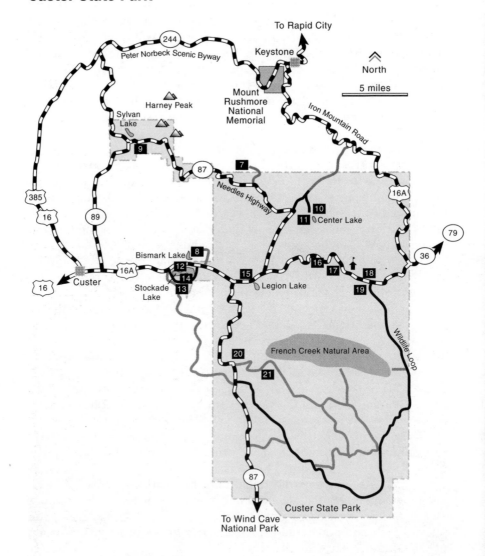

Sylvan Lake Campground
Camping inside Custer State Park's playground

Map	Page 100
Usage	High
Sites	39
Cost	$20 ($24 with electric). A daily park entrance fee or annual pass is also required.
Camp Facilities	Fire rings, picnic tables, water, electric hookups, restrooms, showers, trash containers
Spur Length	Medium—up to 30 feet
Managing Agency	South Dakota Game, Fish and Parks; a host is on site
Reservations	Required—check www.campsd.com or call (800) 710-2267
Season	Open late May through mid-September
Elevation	6,200 feet
GPS Coordinates	N43° 50.42' W103° 33.45'

The Camp

The Sylvan Lake area in the northwest corner of Custer State Park has it all. First there is the lake itself, built in 1881, which is ideal for swimming, fishing, or just paddling across placid waters. The huge granite rocks that hold these waters serve as a beautiful backdrop for photographers and

Sylvan Lake

picnickers. The backside of these rocks is used for technical rock climbing. For hikers, the area is among the region's best. The foot trail around the lake is worth every step. Other trails are just as good and lead to places such as Harney Peak (7,242 feet), South Dakota's highest summit. If you're exploring by car, you need not go far; Sylvan Lake is right along the acclaimed Needles Highway and its most photographed attractions. You also won't need to travel far for convenience and comfort. The Sylvan Lake Lodge next to the lake offers a restaurant, café, lodging, chapel, general store, lounge, and watercraft rentals.

Sylvan Lake Campground

With such grand scenery and so many things to do, it's no wonder that Sylvan Lake Campground is a wildly popular spot in the park. Although the camp is about a half mile southeast of the lake and has no views of the water, that bothers few who stay here. In fact, if you want to secure a spot, you'll need to make reservations well in advance.

This is the park's highest campground and the elevation is evident in the thick forest of spruce and pine. Campsites are packed closely together, but this lush flora makes decent privacy between them. The shadowy forest also gives the camp a more rugged wilderness sense to it—a completely different feel than many other camps in the Black Hills that have open parks and picked-clean forests.

The camp has two sections—a lower loop and a single lane that leads to a higher tent camping area where there are ten walk-in sites. This is a compact arrangement, and getting turned around can be troublesome if you're driving or towing a long camping rig. The best options are tents, pickup campers, and short trailers and motorhomes.

The camp road is paved and there are electric hookups at all the regular campsites. A log-style restroom and shower house is centrally located in the lower loop. Individual campsites vary widely. The longer ones are designated for RV use, while others are open to just tent campers. To find the site that best suits you, check the reservation website which includes detailed information and a photo for each site.

Field Notes

If you are bringing a trailer, you'll need to be good at parking it as most of the back-in spurs are squeezed between trees along a camp road that is narrow and curvy. Not all of the spurs are straight or level.

Directions

From the east side of Custer, turn north on Sylvan Lake Road (HWY 89) and drive north for 6 miles. Turn right onto HWY 87 and follow this road for a half mile to reach the campground on the right. If you're driving a motorhome or driving a trailer, you should use this route as it avoids the narrow tunnels on the Needles Highway.

To reach the campground from Hill City (smaller vehicles only), drive south on HWY 16/HWY 385 for 3 miles and turn left onto HWY 87 (Needles Highway). Drive 6.3 miles on this curvy, narrow road.

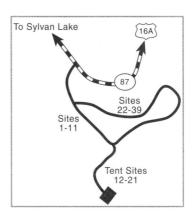

10 Center Lake Non-Profit Youth Camp
Shoreline camping for non-profit youth organizations

Map	Page 100
Usage	High
Sites	5
Cost	$.50 per person with a $6 minimum. A daily park entrance fee or annual pass is also required.
Camp Facilities	Fire rings, picnic tables, water, pit toilets; water and showers are available at Center Lake Campground
Spur Length	Not applicable—tents only
Managing Agency	South Dakota Game, Fish and Parks
Reservations	Required—check www.campsd.com or call (800) 710-2267
Season	Open late May to early September
Elevation	4,700 feet
GPS Coordinates	N43° 48.2' W103° 25.08'

The Camp

This youth camp is found along the northern shore of Center Lake, one of Custer State Park's more secluded lakes. The camp is available to non-profit organizations. Adult supervision is required and only tent camping is permitted. The camp is tucked into the ponderosa pine forest. Though there is a pit toilet, picnic tables, and fire rings, there is no water. You can get water and showers at the main Center Lake Campground.

Center Lake Non-Profit Youth Camp

Center Lake –Katy Walsh photo

Field Notes
This is a prime location for a youth gathering. The lake offers fishing and boating and there is a nearby hiking trail along Grace Coolidge Creek.

Directions
From Custer, drive east on HWY 16A for 7.3 miles. Turn left on HWY 87 (Needles Highway) and follow it north for 3 miles. Turn right onto FR 753 and drive .7 miles to camp turnoff on the right. Follow this road a short distance to the recreation area.

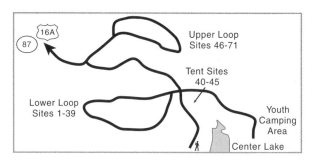

11 Center Lake Campground
Off the beaten path in Custer State Park

Map	Page 100
Usage	High
Sites	71
Cost	$18. A daily park entrance fee or annual pass is also required.
Camp Facilities	Fire rings, picnic tables, water, pit toilets, restrooms, showers, trash containers, boat ramps, amphitheater, pay phone, swim beach
Spur Length	Short to Medium—20 to 30 feet
Managing Agency	South Dakota Game, Fish and Parks; a host is on site
Reservations	Accepted (same day reservations)—check www.campsd.com or call (800) 710-2267
Season	Open early May through September
Elevation	4,700 feet
GPS Coordinates	N43° 48.23' W103° 25.16'

The Camp

Center Lake Campground is in north central Custer State Park. Its out-of-the-way location minimizes drive-by traffic to make it one of the quieter camps in the park. Still, it's easy to reach the park's northern attractions, such as the Needles Highway and Black Hills Playhouse. This is also a destination campground—that is, one at which you may want to stay during the day as well as during the night—and its popularity is justified.

Center Lake Campground –Katy Walsh photo

The campground has two loops that are separated by a good distance. Both of these are under a shady forest of ponderosa pine with some oak trees and rock outcroppings. There is not much understory in this forest, and privacy is limited especially when the camp is full. The other side of the lake includes a third camping area, but this is designated as a campsite for non-profit youth organizations.

The first 45 sites are found in the Lower Loop, which is closer to the lake, showers, and amphitheater. Nearly all of these campsites are best suited for tent camping and a few of them are designated only for tents. The Upper Loop has similar sites—plenty of good tenting options with only a few longer parking spurs for short trailers, such as pop-up campers. Many sites include tent platforms and a few pull-throughs are also available.

Center Lake operates under a system called same day reservations. You can either reserve a campsite (via phone or website) beginning at 7am on the day that you'll be arriving, or you can drive to the campground to find an open campsite, and then call to confirm its availability. If you reserve a site, you must occupy it by 10pm that same day.

The area has plenty of recreational activities. The lake offers a swim beach, fishing for rainbow trout, and boating (there is a no wake rule). The west side of the lake also includes a trailhead for the Grace Coolidge Walk-In Fishing Area. This is a 3-mile trail that follows Grace Coolidge Creek southward toward a campground of the same name. The trail crosses the stream numerous times, which can be difficult if water levels are high.

If you run out of things to do around camp, you have two nearby options. The first is the Black Hills Playhouse, just west of the campground. This roughly 300-seat facility features live theatrical and musical performances. Reservations are recommended if you want to get in to a show. The second option is the Legion Lake Lodge, which is 5 miles to the south. Located next to Legion Lake, this resort features a restaurant, cabins, playground, beach, watercraft rentals, and store.

Field Notes

Although this campground gets busy, it feels like a quiet retreat compared to other campgrounds in the park that are adjacent to noisy highways.

Directions

From Custer, drive east on HWY 16A for 7.3 miles. Turn left on HWY 87 (Needles Highway) and follow it north for 3 miles. Turn right onto FR 753 and drive .7 miles to a turnoff on the right. Follow this road a short distance to the recreation area.

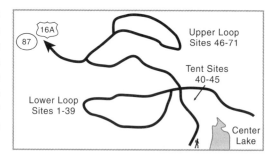

12 Stockade Lake North Campground
Large camp on north side of Stockade Lake

Map	Page 100
Usage	High
Sites	42
Cost	$20 ($24 with electric). A daily park entrance fee or annual pass is also required.
Camp Facilities	Fire rings, picnic tables, water, electric hookups, restrooms, pit toilets, showers, trash containers, playground, amphitheater
Spur Length	Long—up to 65 feet
Managing Agency	South Dakota Game, Fish and Parks; a host is on site
Reservations	Required—check www.campsd.com or call (800) 710-2267
Season	Open late May through September
Elevation	5,280 feet
GPS Coordinates	N43° 46.29' W103° 31.35'

The Camp
Stockade Lake North is an easy-to-reach camp located just four miles east of the town of Custer along the Custer State Park boundary. The location is one of convenience—near town, close to Stockade Lake, along the Peter Norbeck Scenic Byway, and just minutes from a few historical markers

Stockade Lake North Campground

and monuments. It's also a very accommodating campground—if you can drive it here, you can park it here. A paved camp road lined with long parking spurs makes this an ideal camp for those towing long trailers or piloting big RVs.

The camp is in a forest of skinny ponderosa pine. It has been thinned enough that there isn't much privacy between campsites, but there is still decent shade at most. Campsites are positioned on both the inside and outside of two loops. Many of the outer sites are spacious and have huge backyards—plenty of space to spread out behind your parking spur. Others are packed closer together and work well for those who are camping with multiple families or groups.

The first loop is a large, sloping half-mile lane that surrounds a grassy park where there is a playground and amphitheater. The second loop is much smaller and more heavily timbered. These are prime sites that fill up quickly as campers enjoy more privacy and shade.

Stockade Lake is a tenth of a mile away from the campground and the forest blocks views of the water. There is no direct route to the water from the camp, but you can hike to it through the trees. A road directly east of the campground leads to a day-use area. The lake holds crappie, perch, bass, northern pike, and trout.

Even further east, you'll find a road that encircles the lake and offers access to a picnic area, boat ramp, Stockade Lake South Campground, and the Stockade Lake Trail, a 1.5-mile loop.

Field Notes

This campground is another personal favorite of mine. With a playground and large grassy park, this is a great family camp that makes a good base for exploring the Black Hills. Just be sure to get back to camp for the evening program at the amphitheater.

Directions

From Custer, take HWY 16A east for 3.8 miles and turn right.

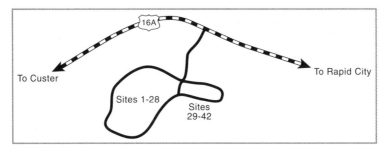

13 Stockade Lake South Campground
Tucked away camp in the forested hills south of Stockade Lake

Map	Page 100
Usage	High
Sites	23; 13 cabins
Cost	$20 ($24 with electric); $37-$47 for cabins. A daily park entrance fee or annual pass is also required.
Camp Facilities	Fire rings, picnic tables, water, electric hookups, restrooms, showers, trash containers
Spur Length	Short to medium—20 to 30 feet
Managing Agency	South Dakota Game, Fish and Parks; a host is on site
Reservations	Required—check www.campsd.com or call (800) 710-2267
Season	Open late May through September
Elevation	5,250 feet
GPS Coordinates	N43˚ 45.84' W103˚ 31.42'

The Camp
Aside from a group area, Stockade Lake has two campgrounds, a large one on the north side along HWY 16A, and this smaller one that is tucked away in the rugged country south of the lake. If you're comparing the two, you'll find that Stockade Lake South has more shade, rock outcrops, shorter parking spurs, cabins, and a more secluded feel. Like the northern camp, there is no direct access to the lake, though it can be reached with a short walk.

Stockade Lake South Campground

The campsites are arranged around a single loop in uneven terrain. A few of these are designated only for tents. Others have short to medium sized parking spurs that work best for tents or small campers like pop-up trailers and short motorhomes. As usual, the sites on the outside of the loop are more spacious than those squeezed into the inside. Many of the campsites have a unique stone fireplace. These were constructed by the Civilian Conservation Corps (CCC) in the 1930s.

A single lane on the south side of the camp stretches uphill to reach an additional three campsites as well as 13 cabins. Each cabin can accommodate four to five people and includes beds, a porch, picnic table, fire ring, electricity, heating, and air conditioning. What you don't get is bedding, a kitchen, or a bathroom. These cabins open up the possibilities of who may join you on your camping trip. You could invite along a party who has no desire to sleep on the ground out in the elements—say new parents with an infant or grandparents.

Reaching the lake from the campground requires a walk of at least a quarter mile, but the southern shore has rugged places that are not easily reached. For the best fishing access, follow the main road over the lake's dam to the east shore where there is a day-use area including a hiking trail and boat ramp. The lake holds crappie, perch, bass, northern pike, and trout.

Follow the main road to the west toward Custer, and you'll find the Gordon Stockade, the lake's namesake. This is a replica of the log fortress that was built in 1874 to help protect against Indian attacks. Interpretive signs at the site tell more of the area's history.

Field Notes

With a few exceptions, Custer State Park specifies the camping spurs here to be just 20 to 25 feet long. I found most of them to be much longer. However, due to the campground's tight and sloping configuration, it would be difficult to fit larger units into the spots. If you're wondering if your rig will fit, save yourself the trouble and choose a site at Stockade Lake North Campground instead.

Directions

From Custer, drive east on HWY 16A for 3 miles. Bear right onto Stockade Lake Drive and drive a little over a half mile to the camp turnoff on the right.

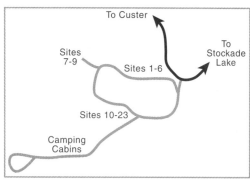

14 Stockade Lake Group Camp
Group campground on the southern shore of Stockade Lake

Map	Page 100
Usage	High
Sites	1 (up to 40 people)
Cost	$6 per person; $120 minimum. A daily park entrance fee or annual pass is also required.
Camp Facilities	Fire rings, group picnic shelter, water, electric, pit toilets, trash containers; showers and restrooms are available in nearby Stockade Lake South Campground
Spur Length	Short—up to 20 feet
Managing Agency	South Dakota Game, Fish and Parks
Reservations	Required—check www.campsd.com or call (800) 710-2267
Season	Open late May through September
Elevation	5,200 feet
GPS Coordinates	N43° 45.99' W103° 31.19'

The Camp

The Stockade Lake Group Camp is an exclusive group campground on the south shore of a large lake. The site is located at the end of its own quarter-mile road, creating a private and secluded spot that is separate from other public facilities. The camp is a gravel loop surrounded by ponderosa pine. The middle of the loop is grass with fire rings, a group sitting area, and a covered picnic shelter with lights and electric outlets.

Stockade Lake Group Camp Area

Stockade Lake

The site is ideal for tent camping, but you can also fit short trailers here too. What you bring depends largely on your group. If you have a small party and expect little traffic, you could fit a few larger units around the loop road. Larger groups with more traffic will want to stick with tents or smaller rigs to keep the road clear and accessible.

Of the three camping areas around Stockade Lake, this one is the closest to the water and is just a short walk to the shore. Anglers will find crappie, perch, bass, northern pike, and trout in these waters. There is a boat ramp on the lake's east side along with a short hiking trail.

Field Notes

This is a great camp for those small organizations or youth groups who want exclusive use of a campground with easy access to a lake. The park offers naturalist programs in the evening.

Directions

From Custer, drive east on HWY 16A for 3 miles. Bear right onto a Stockade Lake Drive a little over a half mile to the turnoff on the left and then drive down the short lane to reach the camp.

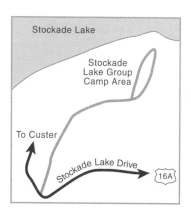

Map	Page 100
Usage	High
Sites	23
Cost	$20 ($24 with electric). A daily park entrance fee or annual pass is also required.
Camp Facilities	Fire rings, picnic tables, water, electric hookups, restrooms, showers, trash containers
Spur Length	Long—up to 60 feet
Managing Agency	South Dakota Game, Fish and Parks; a host is on site
Reservations	Required—check www.campsd.com or call (800) 710-2267
Season	Open late May through September
Elevation	5,050 feet
GPS Coordinates	N43° 45.77' W103° 27.91'

The Camp

Legion Lake is a roadside campground in Custer State Park that will fit large RVs and trailers, though it is also very popular with tent campers. Unlike some other park campgrounds that have a direct view of the highway, this camp is partly separated from the road by a short pine-covered rise. You'll still hear the traffic, but you'll mostly be out of view.

Legion Lake Campground

The camp consists of a tight, paved loop in a grassy park. The campsites on the northern half of the loop have no trees and are packed tightly together in the grass. These make great stargazing spots. The sites on the southern half of the loop sit at the edge of a pine forest where there is some shade, depending on the time of day. Except for a handful of campsites at the ends of the loop, all of the parking spurs face the inside of the park toward each other. This makes it crowded and you'll have very little privacy, especially when the campground is busy. It's not unusual for tents to be pitched just several feet from each other.

There is a trailhead at the western end of the loop for the Legion Lake Trail, a 1.5-mile loop open to foot, hoof, and mountain bike traffic. This loop includes a separate track that ties in to the Centennial Trail, a 111-mile path that traverses the Black Hills.

Legion Lake, the camp's namesake, is located directly across the highway from the campground. A fishing dock close to the camp has a good view over the lake. The Legion Lake Lodge is also within walking distance. The resort has a restaurant, cabins, general store, playground, and beach. The lodge rents watercraft, such as paddle boats, if you need to beat the summer heat by getting out on the water.

Field Notes

If you prefer some privacy at your campsite, look elsewhere. There were only a handful of occupied sites when I stayed here and I still had a tent within 10 feet of my campsite. For ten hours, I heard every word and sound that came from that tent. Truth is, I never intended to stay here, but the camp host was so friendly and inviting, that I couldn't say no.

Directions

From Custer, drive east on HWY 16A for 7 miles to the camp on the left. If driving from Rapid City, drive south on HWY 79 for 15.5 miles to HWY 36 (just past Hermosa). Turn right on HWY 36 and drive westward for 18 miles.

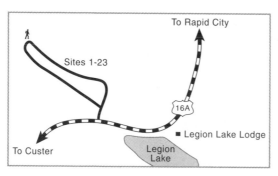

Shady Rest Non-Profit Youth Camp
Primitive camping for non-profit youth organizations

Map	Page 100
Usage	High
Sites	4
Cost	$.50 per person with a $6 minimum. A daily park entrance fee or annual pass is also required.
Camp Facilities	Fire rings, picnic tables, pit toilets, trash containers
Spur Length	Not applicable—tents only
Managing Agency	South Dakota Game, Fish and Parks
Reservations	Required—check www.campsd.com or call (800) 710-2267
Season	Open late May to early September
Elevation	6,000 feet
GPS Coordinates	N43° 46.64' W103° 24.9'

The Camp
Shady Rest is a picnic area in north central Custer State Park. The area is hidden in a mixed forest, right in the middle of a curve along the Peter Norbeck Scenic Byway (HWY 16).

The picnic area is open to anyone, but camping is only available to non-profit youth organizations (adult supervision is required). There are just four sites here for parking, but there is plenty of room to pitch tents.

Shady Rest Non-Profit Youth Camp

The camp is primitive and only tent camping is permitted. Unlike the nearby developed campgrounds, there is no electricity, water, showers, or comfortable restrooms. However, campers can get showers at Game Lodge Campground during the afternoon hours. If your group needs more developed facilities, check out the youth camping area at Center Lake Campground. That site has closer access to potable water and showers.

Field Notes
You'll find a rugged dirt track that climbs the hill south of the camp. Follow it a short distance and you'll gain the ridgetop where there is a terrific view across Custer State Park.

Directions
From Custer, drive east on HWY 16A for 10.2 miles to the camp on the right. If driving from Rapid City, drive south on HWY 79 for 15.5 miles to HWY 36 (just past Hermosa). Turn right on HWY 36 and drive westward for 14.6 miles.

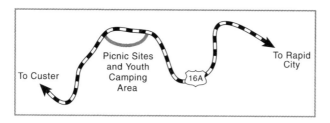

17 Grace Coolidge Campground
Base camp near a walk-in fishing area and area attractions

Map	Page 100
Usage	High
Sites	27
Cost	$20 ($24 with electric). A daily park entrance fee or annual pass is also required.
Camp Facilities	Fire rings, picnic tables, water, electric hookups, restrooms, showers, trash containers, pay phone
Spur Length	Long—up to 60 feet
Managing Agency	South Dakota Game, Fish and Parks; a host is on site
Reservations	Required—check www.campsd.com or call (800) 710-2267
Season	Open late May through September
Elevation	4,360 feet
GPS Coordinates	N43° 46.63' W103° 24.14'

The Camp
You'll find Grace Coolidge Campground in north central Custer State Park along the Peter Norbeck Scenic Byway (HWY 16A). This isn't a hideaway where you'll spend your time in a secluded forest. Rather, it's a convenient base from which you can zip off to the park's main attractions.

Grace Coolidge Campground

The main section of the campground is designed for RVs and trailers. The arrangement is a simple triangular-shaped loop. The long side of this loop is in direct view of the highway and three of the sites have no trees. The other two sides are tucked into a stand of oak near a small brook. The sites are a mix of pull-throughs and back-in spurs.

If you're tent camping, you'll be on the other side of the highway where a gravel pullout has six tent sites. A pit toilet and water are available on this side of the road, but a walk to the main campground is in order for showers and restrooms.

Also on the north side of the highway is a hiking trail that enters the Grace Coolidge Walk-In Fishing Area. This 3-mile trail follows Grace Coolidge Creek northward through a valley to Center Lake Campground. The trail crosses the stream numerous times, which can be difficult if water levels are high.

Less than 2 miles east of the camp, you'll find the Peter Norbeck Visitor Center, which is worth a visit. The State Game Lodge is also just a few minutes away. There, you'll find a restaurant, lounge, general store, chapel, and lodging. For recreational activities, they offer mountain bike rentals, a fly-fishing guiding service, and Buffalo Safari Jeep Rides with a chuckwagon cookout.

Field Notes

This is Custer State Park at your doorstep. While the camp itself offers nothing spectacular, its central location makes it easy to explore both the northern and southern portions of the park as well as more distant attractions such as Mount Rushmore and Wind Cave National Park.

Directions

From Custer, drive east on HWY 16A for 11.5 miles to the camp on the right. If driving from Rapid City, drive south on HWY 79 for 15.5 miles to HWY 36 (just past Hermosa). Turn right on HWY 36 and drive westward for 13.7 miles.

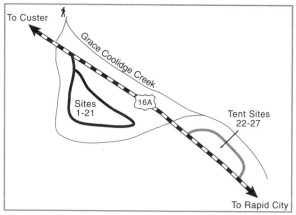

18 Game Lodge Group Camping Area
Group camp on the east side of Custer State Park

Map	Page 100
Usage	High
Sites	8; tent area (up to 100 people)
Cost	$6 per person ($120 minimum). A daily park entrance fee or annual pass is also required.
Camp Facilities	Fire rings, picnic shelter, water, electric hookups, restrooms, showers, trash containers, pay phone
Spur Length	Long—up to 50 feet
Managing Agency	South Dakota Game, Fish and Parks
Reservations	Required—check www.campsd.com or call (800) 710-2267
Season	Open mid-May through September
Elevation	4,150 feet
GPS Coordinates	N43° 45.70' W103° 22.12'

The Camp

The Game Lodge Group Camping Area is found across the highway from Game Lodge Campground on the east side of Custer State Park. This exclusive group camp is a scenic one. Deciduous trees shroud the sides of the camp's verdant park, and conifers line the adjacent ridgetops above a rock cliff. Grace Coolidge Creek flows through the camp where it fills a pond. A footbridge spans the creek so you can reach a picnic area.

Game Lodge Group Camping Area

The camp has a single loop road that accesses two camping areas. The first is an RV and trailer area with eight electric sites. Next to this is a large, grassy tent area near the pond. The campground also offers a covered picnic area and restrooms. Although there is enough space for up to 100 campers, parking is limited so carpooling is wise.

From the campground, it's less than a quarter mile to the east to reach the park's Wildlife Loop Road. The scenic Iron Mountain Road is only a couple miles to the east, too, and heads northward toward Keystone and Mount Rushmore. Head west and you'll reach the Needles Highway in less than 6 miles.

If your group needs more lodging, supplies, or gear, send them to the State Game Lodge just a quarter mile to the west. This resort includes a restaurant, lounge, general store, chapel, and cozy accommodations. For recreational activities, they offer mountain bike rentals, a fly-fishing guiding service, and Buffalo Safari Jeep Rides with a chuckwagon cookout.

Field Notes
Bighorn sheep and wild turkeys are common visitors to the camp.

Directions
From Custer, drive east on HWY 16A for 13.6 miles to the camp on the left. If driving from Rapid City, drive south on HWY 79 for 15.5 miles to HWY 36 (just past Hermosa). Turn right on HWY 36 and drive westward for 11.8 miles.

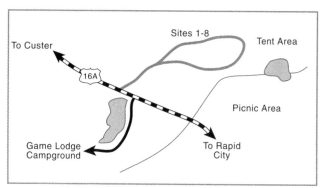

19 Game Lodge Campground
Well-equipped highway camp on the east side of Custer State Park

Map	Page 100
Usage	High
Sites	56 sites; 11 cabins
Cost	$16-$24; $47 for cabins. A daily park entrance fee or annual pass is also required.
Camp Facilities	Fire rings, picnic tables, water, electric hookups, restrooms, pit toilets, showers, trash containers, laundromat, theater, dump station, pay phone, playground
Spur Length	Long—up to 60 feet
Managing Agency	South Dakota Game, Fish and Parks; a host is on site
Reservations	Required during peak season—check www.campsd.com or call (800) 710-2267
Season	Open all year
Elevation	4,175 feet
GPS Coordinates	N43° 45.68' W103° 22.48'

The Camp

Game Lodge Campground is on the east side of Custer State Park, sandwiched between a wooded hill and the Peter Norbeck Scenic Byway (HWY 16A). From the road, it doesn't look a whole lot different than any other campground. But this isn't an ordinary camp—this is the park's

Game Lodge Campground

premiere camping spot that rivals many private campgrounds. With impressive on-site facilities and close-by services, this is a camp where you can settle in for an extended stay.

The camp is sprawled out along an open park right along the busy highway. There are few trees, just some short deciduous ones, and shade is nearly non-existent. Privacy is impossible. Why would anyone want to stay here? To start, Grace Coolidge Creek runs along the back of the camp and 17 sites sit along the brook. Then there is the thick, lush grass—city park like—that blankets the ground throughout the camp. It's perfect for pitching a tent, playing, or practicing your fishing cast. There are also those features that make this a great family camp, like a pond to fish or swim in, a playground to play on, and a theater where there are naturalist programs in the evening. An on-site dump station, showers, and laundromat also make it easy to keep camping. For more services, you'll find State Game Lodge just a quarter mile to the west. This resort includes a restaurant, lounge, general store, chapel, and lodging. For recreational activities, they offer mountain bike rentals, a fly-fishing guiding service, and Buffalo Safari Jeep Rides with a chuckwagon cookout.

The camp's parking spurs are long, level, and paved. For tent campers, there are more than a dozen tent-only sites, most of which are along the creek. For those who don't have an RV or a tent, there are 11 rentable cabins. These come with beds, fire rings, electricity, heating, air conditioning and a porch. You'll need to bring your own outdoor cooking gear and bedding.

It's easy to explore the area from here. The park's Wildlife Loop Road begins just a tenth of a mile to the east. Likewise, the scenic Iron Mountain Road is only a couple miles to the east and heads northward toward Keystone and Mount Rushmore. Head west and you'll reach the Needles Highway in 6 miles.

Field Notes

There were bighorn sheep in the camp during my visit. I was told that wild turkeys and bison can also be expected. I found the camp to be almost full on a Tuesday night in late September—make reservations!

Directions

From Custer, drive east on HWY 16A for 13.7 miles. If driving from Rapid City, drive south on HWY 79 for 15.5 miles to HWY 36 (just past Hermosa). Turn right on HWY 36 and drive westward for 11.7 miles.

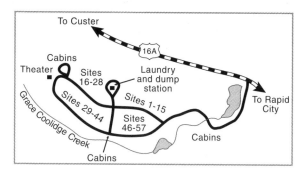

20 Blue Bell Campground
A camp of comfort and convenience on the west side of Custer State Park

Map	Page 100
Usage	High
Sites	31; 23 cabins
Cost	$20 ($24 with electric); $37-$47 for cabins. A daily park entrance fee or annual pass is also required.
Camp Facilities	Fire rings, picnic tables, water, electric hookups, restrooms, showers, trash containers, amphitheater, pay phone
Spur Length	Medium to long—30 to 40 feet
Managing Agency	South Dakota Game, Fish and Parks; a host is on site
Reservations	Required during peak season—check www.campsd.com or call (800) 710-2267
Season	Open late April through October
Elevation	4,900 feet
GPS Coordinates	N43° 43.1' W103° 28.91'

The Camp

The Blue Bell area is named for an executive of Bell Telephone who built the nearby lodge on the west side of Custer State Park. Campers who stay here at the campground are often interested in horseback riding, exploring the park's open spaces and wildlife, stream fishing, and staying a little bit off the beaten path without sacrificing comfort or conveniences.

Blue Bell Campground

The area is covered in tall ponderosa pines making this one of Custer's most shaded camps. Grassy groundcover makes comfortable tent spots. The camp features a paved loop road as well as paved parking spurs. Campsite numbers can be confusing as four sites are replaced by parking pads for four cabins. As a result, you'll find sites that are out of order (site 5 is next to 8) and higher than expected numbers (there is a site 34 even though there are only 31 in the camp). Of these sites, four of them are designated only for tent use. The others will accommodate medium-sized trailers and motorhomes, which are easy to set up on the level spurs.

A loop just east of the campground includes nearly two-dozen cabins that feature electricity, heating, air conditioning, porches, picnic tables, and fire rings, but no bathrooms. Each cabin can accommodate four to five people, depending on the unit. All you need to bring is your own bedding and outdoor cooking gear.

Regardless of whether you're staying in a cabin or campsite, you'll appreciate the area's services and facilities. Staying true to Custer State Park standards, there are electric hookups, restrooms, and showers in the camp. The nearby lodge takes care of the rest. You'll find a laundromat, restaurant, lounge, wireless Internet, chapel, gas station, and general store. There are also chuckwagon cookouts, guided horse rides, and additional lodging. Naturalist programs are presented in the evenings at the campground amphitheater.

Field Notes

Overall, the camp feels more like a nicely developed city campground than one you'd expect in the rugged Black Hills.

Directions

From Custer, drive east on HWY 16A for 6.2 miles to HWY 87. Use caution—this is an abrupt stop around a blind curve. Drive south on HWY 87 for 4.7 miles to the camp turnoff on the left.

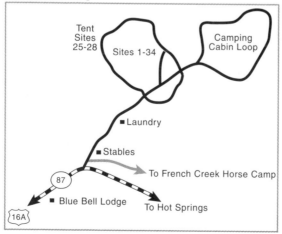

21 French Creek Horse Camp
Custer State Park's horse campground

Map	Page 100
Usage	High
Sites	28; 3 cabins
Cost	$23-$27; $47 for cabins. A daily park entrance fee or annual pass is also required.
Camp Facilities	Fire rings, picnic tables, water, electric hookups, restrooms, pit toilets, showers, trash containers, pay phone, corrals
Spur Length	Long—up to 100 feet
Managing Agency	South Dakota Game, Fish and Parks; a host is on site
Reservations	Required during peak season—check www.campsd.com or call (800) 710-2267
Season	Open all year, except cabins which are open May through October
Elevation	4,650 feet
GPS Coordinates	N43° 42.83' W103° 27.47'

The Camp
If you're coming to ride your horse in Custer State Park, this is your campground. Located on the west side of the park, the French Creek Horse Camp has access to numerous horse trails as well the 111-mile Centennial Trail.

French Creek Horse Camp

There are a few requirements and rules for staying in this campground. First, you must have horses. Secondly, your animals must meet certain requirements, such as testing negative for swamp fever within the last year and being checked by a brand inspector. You'll also need to keep your corral clean, use weed-free feed (started three days prior to arrival), and not leave horses unattended overnight. Details on these rules are available on the reservation website, but you can also consult the camp host for more information.

The campground consists of two separate loops that occupy a small mountain valley along the banks of French Creek. A thin stand of pine trees creates partial shade for most of the campsites, though some are under the open sky. Each site includes electric hookups and a corral for your animals. If you need more space, you can rent an additional corral when you arrive.

The first loop is a narrow one that receives the most shade. Behind it are two campsites (sites A and B) that are operated on a first come, first served basis. The second loop is found next to the trailhead and three rentable cabins. These cabins come equipped with beds, electricity, heating, air conditioning, porches, picnic tables, and fire rings, but no bathrooms. Each cabin can accommodate four people. You provide your own bedding and outdoor cooking gear.

The nearby Blue Bell Lodge, 2 miles to the west, has a laundromat, restaurant, lounge, wireless Internet, chapel, gas station, general store, and chuckwagon cookouts.

Field Notes

If this camp is full (and it is sometimes reserved out months before summer), check out the Iron Creek Horse Camp or Willow Creek Horse Camp, both of which are operated by the Forest Service. Both camps have fewer services, but access a good network of trails around the Black Elk Wilderness.

Directions

From Custer, drive east on HWY 16A for 6.2 miles to HWY 87. Use caution—this is an abrupt stop around a blind curve. Drive south on HWY 87 for 4.7 miles to the Blue Bell area. Turn left onto North Lame Johnny Road and follow it 2 miles to the campground.

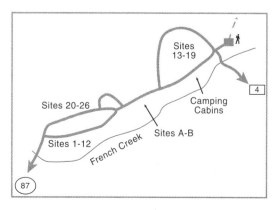

French Creek Natural Area

Want a backcountry campsite? The central part of Custer State Park includes the 2,200-acre French Creek Natural Area. This is a primitive, undeveloped section of land traversed only by a crude 12-mile trail that runs along a meandering east-to-west drainage. Backcountry camping is allowed anywhere within the natural area and there are also two designated backcountry campsites along the trail that you can choose. These include a flat spot to pitch a tent and a primitive pit toilet. A backcountry camping permit for the natural area costs $4 per person. You can register and pay at the trailhead. The western trailhead is at French Creek Horse Camp. The eastern trailhead is located along the eastern half of the Wildlife Loop Road.

A few notes of caution are in order. This isn't an easy path to hike from end to end. It's not marked or maintained and there are places that are indistinct. The rule of thumb here is to parallel French Creek to stay on course. You'll also encounter poison ivy, rattlesnakes, around 40 creek crossings, and a section on the east side called the Narrows where a short 100-foot swim—or a 60-foot steep canyon climb—is required to get through it. The reward is experiencing a truly wild part of Custer that is both beautiful and enchanting.

Rock cliffs in the French Creek Natural Area

Wind Cave National Park

Wind Cave National Park is located on the southeastern edge of the Black Hills where rugged, mountainous terrain transitions to rolling prairies of tall grass. The highlight of this nearly 30,000-acre reserve is a huge and complex cave system that ranks as the fourth largest in the world. More than 135 miles of passages have been mapped here and the exploration continues.

If you want to explore these caverns yourself, you can take one of the underground tours that the park conducts. Most of these run around two hours or less. If the underworld is not for you, you can opt to spend your time at the visitor center, hike along some of the 30 miles of park trails, or watch the entertaining antics of a prairie dog colony.

---

22 Elk Mountain Campground
Quiet and large camp at Wind Cave National Park

Map	Page 80
Usage	Moderate
Sites	75; 2 group sites
Cost	$12 ($6 during the off season)
Camp Facilities	Fire rings, picnic tables, water, restrooms, pit toilets, trash containers
Spur Length	Long—up to 50 feet
Managing Agency	National Park Service —Wind Cave National Park; a host is on site
Reservations	Only group sites can be reserved—check www.nps.gov/wica or call (605) 745-4600.
Season	Open all year
Elevation	4,300 feet
GPS Coordinates	N43° 33.96' W103° 29.77'

The Camp

Wind Cave National Park's only campground, Elk Mountain, is a large one that rarely approaches capacity. Several loops of campsites are stretched out over a half mile along the edge of a ponderosa pine forest. The first loop is the most rugged and includes 21 small tent sites on a short, timbered rise. Loop B and its 22 sunny sites are nearby on the other side of the paved camp road. Next comes a series of pull-throughs that line both sides of the main road. These are prime spots if you're not good at backing into a spur. Loop C, favored by tent campers, includes a dozen sites including a walk-in spot. A few of these have decent shade. Loop D is found at the far end of the campground and includes the last 17 spaces. There are no trees in this loop and you'll get plenty of sun. Longer RVs or trailers are best suited for Loop B, Loop D, or the pull-through sites where the parking spurs are longer and more level.

Elk Mountain Campground

The park offers two group sites in Loop D for parties ranging from 9 to 30 people. These are only available by reservation and requires a $20 non-refundable deposit. Group rates are $1 per person with a $20 minimum.

Other campground features that you'll appreciate include amphitheater programs, recycling bins, firewood for sale, both restrooms and pit toilets, and water faucets between every other site. All of the campground water is turned off during the off-season.

The prairie grass grows waist-high here and is mowed at each campsite. Be careful if you wander about through the tall grass—this is rattlesnake (and bison) country. If you do want to explore by foot, you'll find the 1-mile Elk Mountain Trail, which loops around the western half of the camp.

Field Notes

This is an overlooked camp that is worth a stay. Out of several visits on summer weekends, I've never seen more than a dozen or so campers here.

Directions

From Hot Springs, drive north on HWY 385 for 11.2 miles. Turn left and drive southward for about a half mile. Turn right and drive a final half mile.

To get here from Custer, drive south on HWY 385 for 18.5 miles and turn right.

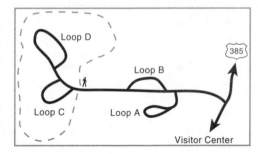

Cold Brook Lake Recreation Site
Popular recreation area on the outskirts of Hot Springs

Map	Page 80
Usage	Moderate
Sites	13
Cost	$5
Camp Facilities	Fire rings, picnic tables, water, pit toilets, trash containers, playground, archery range, boat ramp, picnic shelters
Spur Length	Medium—up to 30 feet
Managing Agency	U.S. Army Corps of Engineers
Reservations	Not accepted—first come, first served
Season	Open mid-May to mid-September (lake is open all year)
Elevation	3,600 feet
GPS Coordinates	N43° 27.69' W103° 29.49'

The Camp

Cold Brook Lake—a reservoir built to control flooding—is part of a popular recreation site on the northern fringe of the town of Hot Springs. The close proximity to South Dakota's twentieth largest populace brings a lot of traffic to the area—dog walkers, joggers, anglers, campers, drivers, partiers, you name it. Though the campground doesn't get the use that the nearby lake does, you'll still have plenty of visitors who pass by.

Cold Brook Lake Campground

The lake itself is about a half mile long and fills a narrow basin that is surrounded by pine-sprinkled hills. The lake offers a beach, boat ramp, and covered picnic shelters. An archery range is located on the east side. On the north end, you'll find a group use area, a designated wildlife area, and the campground.

The campground is situated in the southern end of scenic Cold Brook Canyon, near the mouth of the lake. Flanking one side of the camp is a red cliff and a creek lined with deciduous trees. While these trees and the surrounding pines add interest and beauty, the camp itself is in a grassy park that has little shade.

The campsites are roomy and spaced out along a single loop. The center of the loop includes a horseshoe pit, playground, and space for kids to run. There are plenty of places to pitch tents here, and short trailers or motorhomes will also work well on the level spurs. However, if you're piloting a large RV or dragging a long fifth-wheel, you'll do better at nearby Cottonwood Springs Lake Campground (west of Hot Springs) or Angostura Recreation Area (south of Hot Springs).

Field Notes
A flood siren and an ominous warning sign near the camp's entrance instructs you to seek higher ground during a flood. This is something that you'll think about when you wake up in the middle of the night and hear raindrops on your tent. Also, this is not an access point to the Cold Brook Canyon Trail. That 1.4-mile path is located within Wind Cave National Park, about 7 miles north on HWY 385.

Directions
From the north edge of Hot Springs, drive north about a half mile on HWY 385. Turn left onto Badger Clark Road (CR 87A) and follow it a mile. Turn left onto Cold Brook Road and drive a final 1.5 miles to the recreation area.

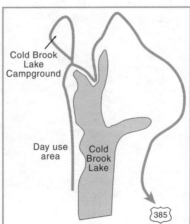

24 Cottonwood Springs Lake Campground
Hilltop camp at the southern end of the Black Hills

Map	Page 80
Usage	Low
Sites	18
Cost	$5
Camp Facilities	Fire rings, picnic tables, water, restrooms, trash containers, playground, boat ramp, picnic shelters
Spur Length	Long—up to 40 feet
Managing Agency	U.S. Army Corps of Engineers
Reservations	Not accepted—first come, first served
Season	Open mid-May to mid-September (lake is open all year)
Elevation	4,025 feet
GPS Coordinates	N43° 26.37' W103° 34.30'

The Camp
Cotton Springs Lake Campground sits on the top of a hill where you can overlook the southern reaches of the Black Hills. The crest of this knoll is crowned with tall lodgepole pine trees, but they only offer shade to a few sites. Privacy between the sites is minimal at best, but the camp is rarely busy so campers can spread out for a little more solitude. The paved parking spurs are found on both sides of a paved loop road. The inside of the loop contains a grassy, open slope with a playground and horseshoe pits.

Cottonwood Springs Lake Campground

On the northern side of the hill is Cottonwood Lake, a tiny reservoir built to help prevent area flooding. Since the campsites are on the south-facing side of the hill, there is no direct view of the lake, which is nearly two hundred vertical feet below the camp.

A separate road leads to the lake, which is a small body of water just 500 feet wide and less than a half mile long. Several covered group picnic shelters are available, as is another playground. A boat ramp gives boaters access to the water, but only electric motors are permitted. There is a designated wildlife area northwest of the lake, on the left side of the road. Here, you'll find a half-mile foot trail that leads through the Cottonwood Springs Creek drainage.

Field Notes

My first mountain lion spotting in the wild was here at this camp. A cougar fixed with a radio collar leisurely walked across an open hillside near the highway, darted across the road, and then headed south into the forest.

Directions

From Hot Springs, drive west on HWY 18 for 3.5 miles and turn north on CR 17. Drive north for 2 miles, following the signs to the campground.

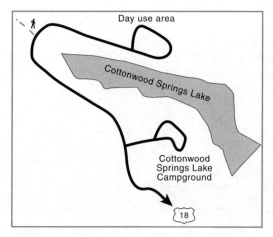

Angostura Recreation Area

Capping the far southern end of the Black Hills, Angostura Recreation Area is an outstanding example of how a reservoir built for irrigation and flood control can double as a premiere site for water sports. It started in 1946 with the construction of the dam, which was finished three years later. The reservoir it created is a large one—4,706 acres with 42 miles of shoreline. Recreation ebbed and flowed through the 1970s and 80s, but has grown steadily since 1991. Today, the reservoir is a regional draw and visitors come here from many different states to camp, boat, water ski, swim, and fish for walleye, crappie, bass, northern pike, bluegill, and perch. They enjoy excellent facilities, a mild climate, scenic views, and proximity to the Black Hills' many attractions.

Angostura Reservoir

25

Angostura Recreation Area Campgrounds
Reservoir camping at its finest at the south end of the Black Hills

Map	Page 80
Usage	High
Sites	168; 10 cabins
Cost	$12 ($16 with electric hookups); $37 for cabins. A daily park entrance fee or annual pass is also required.
Camp Facilities	Fire rings, picnic tables, water, electric hookups, restrooms, showers, trash containers, boat ramps, amphitheater, playgrounds, fish cleaning stations, dump stations, picnic shelters
Spur Length	Long—up to 80 feet
Managing Agency	South Dakota Game, Fish and Parks; multiple hosts are on site
Reservations	Accepted—check www.campsd.com or call (800) 710-2267
Season	Open May through September (lake is open all year)
Elevation	3,200 feet
GPS Coordinates	N43° 20.57' W103° 25.34'

The Camps

There are four campgrounds strung out along the east shoreline of Angostura Reservoir. The northern pair is accessed from the park's north entrance, where you'll also find a scenic overlook, marina and resort, store, disc golf course, boat ramp, boat slips, two beaches, and the park's headquarters with a visitor center. The southern pair of campgrounds and boat ramps is reached

Horseshoe Campground at Angostura Reservoir

from a separate south entrance. Both sides of the park include fish cleaning stations and picnic shelters, some of which have water and electricity. While you can't drive directly from the northern end to the southern end, there is a 1-mile trail that connects the two halves.

Each campground has a playground, pit toilets as well as restrooms, showers, level parking spurs, sites with electric hookups, some double sites, a few handicap-accessible sites, and at least two camping cabins that can be reserved. If you're looking for a specific type of spot, check the reservation website. There you'll find details and a photo for each site so that you know exactly what you are getting.

Starting from the north, the first camp is Cheyenne Campground. This one has a more mountainous feel to it, mostly due to sitting higher above the reservoir in a pine forest. Some of these campsites get full shade, which is highly coveted on hot summer days. The first 14 sites are situated around a single loop. The remaining sites are divided up between three separate areas, which allows for more privacy. Many of these sites do not have electric and are favored by tent campers.

The second campground is Cascade, where you'll find sites 26-89 packed in along three connected loops that receive decent shade from ponderosa pine, oak, and cottonwood trees. This popular camp is right along the shoreline where there is a swim beach. About a dozen sites back against the water. There is also an amphitheater where junior naturalist activities are held for kids aged 7-12. A trail to the southern campgrounds

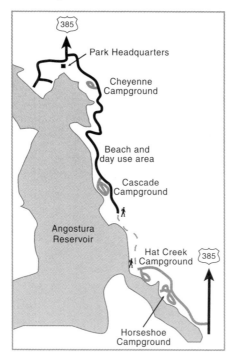

can be reached from this camp by heading south on the road a short distance. I found wild turkeys roaming about the camp.

On the southern end of the recreation area, you'll find Hat Creek Campground. A small loop holds 21 campsites, some of which are along the shoreline. Many of these receive more sun as the trees are not as thick here. The exception is a designated tent camping area with five shaded tent sites.

The last campground is Horsehead. You'll find a sprawling layout here with sites spaced nicely along two loops. Each site has two or three trees so shade can be found, but you'll have to move around as the sun arcs across the sky. From here, you get views of wooded hills to the west. The east skyline consists of a scattering of homes.

Field Notes

Weekends and holidays often fill these campsites. If you prefer a quieter visit, try the middle of the week or an off-month like September.

Directions

From Hot Springs, drive south on HWY 385/HWY 18 for 4.5 miles to reach HWY 79. Turn right here and drive another 2.8 miles south to reach the north entrance. Turn here and follow the signs less than 2 more miles to reach the recreation area and Cascade and Cheyenne campgrounds.

To reach Hat Creek and Horsehead campgrounds at the south entrance, continue south along the highway for another 1.5 miles to the turnoff, and again follow the signs to reach the campgrounds.

Badlands National Park

Badlands National Park is a world of wonder and intrigue among South Dakota's sprawling prairies. In some areas, you'll scan miles of windswept grassland that are roamed by wildlife and covered with wildflowers. In others, you'll navigate through a moonscape of eroded formations that shape colorful spires, pinnacles, buttes, mounds, and toadstools. These badlands are replete with fossils from the distant past. The fossil beds found here are considered among the richest in the world and they have revealed a wide spectrum of now-extinct animals.

Today, the area is still rich with wildlife, though these animals look much different than their ancient predecessors. Throughout the park you'll find roaming bison and pronghorn antelope. Bighorn sheep were re-introduced here as were black-footed ferrets, which were once on the brink of extinction. Thriving off a diet of prairie dogs, these weasel-like animals seem to be recovering nicely in the park's habitat. Other critters you may spot include foxes, coyotes, mule deer, and rattlesnakes.

Badlands National Park is located about forty miles east of the Black Hills. The park is comprised of three units that cover nearly 243,000 acres of land. The Stronghold Unit and Palmer Creek Unit are in the Pine Ridge Indian Reservation. The North Unit—the most popular and developed area of the park—is further north near I-90. The North Unit includes the park's two campgrounds, trailheads, overlooks, headquarters, the paved Badlands Loop Road, and the gravel Sage Creek Rim Road. Whether you come here to camp, venture into the backcountry, or just explore the park by car, you're sure to leave with some worthwhile photographs and memories.

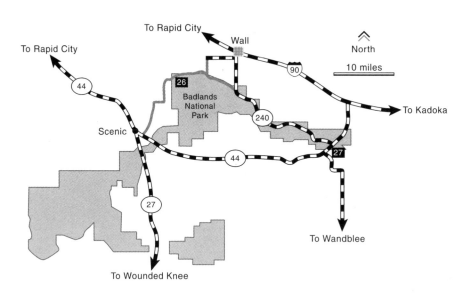

26

Sage Creek Campground
Primitive camping on the savanna in Badlands National Park

Map	Page 139
Usage	Moderate
Sites	21+
Cost	None. A daily park entrance fee or annual pass is required.
Camp Facilities	Covered picnic tables, pit toilets, trash containers, horse hitching posts
Spur Length	Long—unlimited lengths
Managing Agency	National Park Service—Badlands National Park
Reservations	Not accepted—first come, first served
Season	Open all year
Elevation	2,550 feet
GPS Coordinates	N43° 53.65' W102° 24.82'

The Camp

Sage Creek Campground is located in the very northern portion of Badlands National Park near the Badlands Wilderness Area (also known as Sage Creek Wilderness Area). Many people would term this place as remote, desolate, and barren. Yet others find beauty and allure in such undeveloped, semi-arid land.

Sage Creek Campground

The dusty campground occupies a tiny portion of a valley that is surrounded by grassy hills and a spattering of trees. It's scenery that may make you feel like a pioneer out on the plains of middle America with nothing but your wagon. To further this feeling, you'll share some of their same challenges: scarce water, strong winds, intense sunlight and heat (the average summertime high temperature is 88 degrees), powerful storms that can leave roads impassable, bugs that sting, rattlesnakes, and bison that tramp through your camp whenever they want.

The campground has no designated sites. It's nothing more than a loop road, a pair of pit toilets, and 21 scattered picnic tables, 11 of which are covered. The inside of this oval is mostly devoid of grass, so tents get pitched on dirt and bison chips. Those with trailers, vans, and RVs just park somewhere along the road and call it good. Campfires are not permitted.

On the southwest side of the camp, you'll find a designated horse area with hitching posts. National park rules require that riders use weed-free hay or feed, clean up manure, and keep horses picketed and out of the campground loop. The nearest watering hole is CCC Spring, said to be a half mile to the southwest.

So who camps here? A lot of people do, actually. On a late September weekend, I found more than a dozen camping parties here. The camp largely appeals to those who want free camping while traveling toward another destination. It's also favored by backcountry enthusiasts who venture into the primitive hinterlands of the adjacent wilderness area.

Field Notes

If it rains during your stay, you'll have a serious mess on your hands, or feet rather, and boot scrapers are provided at the toilets. Secondly, stargazers will love the big, unspoiled sky here at night.

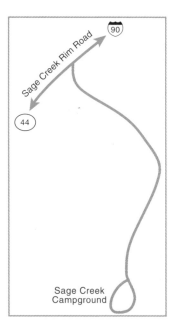

Directions

From Rapid City, head southeast on HWY 44 for 40 miles. Turn north on Sage Creek Road (Road 590) and drive 14 miles to a turnoff on the right. Drive south on the gravel road for 1.2 miles.

To reach the camp from I-90 at Wall, take Exit 110 and head south on HWY 240 for 1.4 miles. Turn right here on Sage Creek Road and follow it for 10 miles to reach the gravel Sage Creek Rim Road. Turn right and follow this gravel road west for almost 5 miles to the camp turnoff on the left. Drive south for 1.2 miles to reach the camp.

27 Cedar Pass Campground
Primary campground on the east side of Badlands National Park

Map	Page 139
Usage	Moderate
Sites	96; 4 group sites
Cost	$15 ($28 for electric). A daily park entrance fee or annual pass is required.
Camp Facilities	Picnic tables, water, electric hookups, restrooms, trash containers, dump station
Spur Length	Long—up to 40 feet
Managing Agency	National Park Service—Badlands National Park; a host is on site
Reservations	Only group sites can be reserved—check www.nps.gov/badl or call (877) 386-4383
Season	Open all year
Elevation	2,400 feet
GPS Coordinates	N43° 44.58' W101° 56.93'

The Camp

Cedar Pass Campground is on the east side of Badlands National Park and is conveniently reached on paved roads from I-90, which is almost 9 miles to the north. Unlike the park's other campground to the west, which is far more primitive, this camp features grand views of the badland formations directly from your campsite. It's also located next to the Ben Reifel Visitor Center, which you should incorporate into your park outing.

Cedar Pass Campground

The campground is comprised of two main loops of individual campsites on a grassy flat. The eastern one, Agate Loop, contains sites 1-39. Just west of it is Butte Loop with sites 40-96. A separate loop near the campground entrance has four group sites that can be reserved. Group camping rates are $3 per person with a $30 minimum.

Campsites are very basic. They include a covered picnic table and lots of wooden posts to keep you from parking on the grass. Parking spurs are level but vary in length and layout; there are some back-in spurs, but most are simple pull-throughs directly along the main loop road. Campfires are not allowed at the sites or anywhere within the park. An amphitheater near the entrance is used for evening programs.

During the peak season, you'll be sweltering here. Average daytime highs during the summer months are 88 degrees, but you'll often be in the 90s. Evenings are comfortably cool with temperatures in the 50s and 60s. However, you can't count on it being hot. It can get frigid here, too, and strong prairie winds can have you huddling inside your shelter.

The campground rarely fills to capacity, but it does get busy here. Easy access from the Interstate, coupled with the natural scenery of this fascinating national park, make it an ideal place to spend a night or two and many campers do just that. If you're looking for a quieter camping experience further off the beaten path, follow the Badlands Loop Road to the northwest. Where the pavement turns to gravel, continue another 12 miles to reach Sage Creek Campground.

Field Notes

Spectacular! The jagged badland spires and pinnacles that fill the northern horizon make this a very unique campground. Camping here gives you the chance to get some great pictures of the formations at sunrise or sunset.

Directions

From I-90 east of Wall, take Exit 131 and turn south onto HWY 240. Drive south for 8.5 miles to reach the campground. To reach the campground from I-90 at Wall, take Exit 110 and drive southward on HWY 240 for 30 miles through the park. If you're driving a big motorhome or towing a long trailer, you'll likely want to take Exit 131.

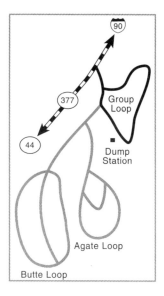

Hikers approach the Harney Peak Lookout in the Black Hills National Forest

WYOMING'S BLACK HILLS

While the Black Hills are usually associated with South Dakota, they also extend into northeastern Wyoming. Wyoming's share includes the Bear Lodge Mountains, a north-south range topping 6,400 feet that is within the Black Hills National Forest.

The difference between these mountains and those found in nearby South Dakota is drastic. On this side of the state line, the Hills' include no amusement parks, casinos, towering rock spires, deep canyons, or sizable reservoirs. Instead, these mountains have gentler terrain that still holds their primitive character—they have far fewer developments and private inholdings. The hills are covered mostly by aspen, ponderosa pine, and tall, thick grasses. Oak and shrubs fill in the gaps, especially in the wetter areas. The land serves as habitat to deer, turkeys, small populations of rarely-seen elk, mountain lions, and many different types of birds. Black bears were once eradicated from this area, but they are now back to some degree with enough signs and sightings to prove their presence.

Recreation within the national forest includes camping, hunting, off-highway driving, and trout fishing. Hiking, mountain biking, and horse riding are also common on a sizable trail system in the southern Bear Lodge Mountains.

By far, the most popular attraction in this corner of Wyoming is Devils Tower, a column of eroding rock that stretches over a thousand feet into the sky. You'll find the tower west of the national forest along the edge of the Black Hills where mountainous terrain transitions to windswept prairies.

Wyoming's Black Hills Campgrounds

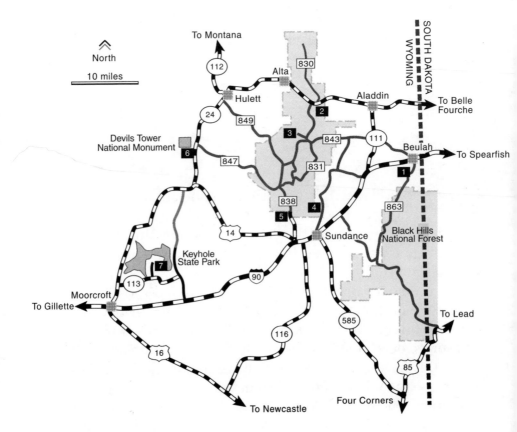

Campground Number	Campground Name	Page Number
1	Sand Creek Public Access Area	147
2	Bearlodge Campground	149
3	Cook Lake Recreation Area	151
4	Sundance Horse Camp	153
5	Reuter Campground	155
6	Belle Fourche Campground (Devils Tower)	157
7	Keyhole State Park Campgrounds	160

■1 Sand Creek Public Access Area
A stream-fishing hideaway near the Wyoming-South Dakota border

Map	Page 146
Usage	Moderate
Sites	24+
Cost	None
Camp Facilities	Fire rings, pit toilets
Spur Length	Long—unlimited lengths
Managing Agency	Wyoming Game and Fish
Reservations	Not accepted—first come, first served
Season	Open all year
Elevation	3,650 feet
GPS Coordinates	N44° 30.89' W104 ° 5.83'

The Camp
This Wyoming Game and Fish Access Area consists of 284 acres and 2 miles of stream fishing next to the Black Hills National Forest. The primitive mile-long camping area is found along spring-fed Sand Creek. Grassy campsites are dispersed, but many of them have stone fire rings and obvious parking spurs. The area is complemented by deciduous trees and colorful canyon walls.

Sand Creek Public Access Area

The adjacent creek is considered one of the best fisheries in Wyoming's Black Hills. It's claimed that between five and six thousand trout (brown, rainbow, and some brook) live in each mile stretch of the stream. There are rattlesnakes along the banks, so watch your step—and children.

Field Notes
This is the locals' hangout, so you might feel a little out of place if you're an obvious tourist.

Directions
From Sundance, take I-90 east for 18 miles to Exit 205 at Beulah. Turn south on the gravel road and drive 2 to 3 miles to one of the numerous turnoffs.

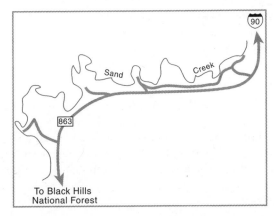

2 Bearlodge Campground
Sleepy camp in a quiet corner of Wyoming

Map	Page 146
Usage	Low
Sites	8
Cost	$10
Camp Facilities	Fire rings, picnic tables, pit toilets, trash containers
Spur Length	Medium—up to 30 feet
Managing Agency	USDA Forest Service—Black Hills National Forest
Reservations	Not accepted—first come, first served
Season	Open late May until snow closure
Elevation	4,700 feet
GPS Coordinates	N44° 39.27' W104° 19.61'

The Camp

Bearlodge Campground is tucked away in Wyoming's sleepiest corner just 13 miles from South Dakota and 24 miles from Montana. The quiet highway here passes through beautiful forests, rolling hills, and fields of hay. Of course in August, when the Sturgis motorcycle rally is underway—and a week before and after—the highway becomes a pipeline for bikers riding between Sturgis and Devils Tower, which is about a half hour's drive west of the camp.

Bearlodge Campground

The campground is a small loop that is concealed by a ponderosa pine forest just a tenth of a mile off the highway. Inside the camp, the trees have been thinned and there isn't a lot of privacy, but none is really needed here as visitation is light. Parking spurs have been improved and made longer, but still don't accommodate the largest of trailers and RVs. The camp works best for tents, pickup campers, and small motorhomes or camping vans.

To make a day trip to the Cook Lake Recreation Area—the chief attraction in the Bear Lodge Mountains with a lake, hiking trails, campground, and picnic area—drive west on HWY 24 for 2 miles and then turn southward on FR 832. Drive 8 miles south on this gravel road. Turn right onto FR 842 and proceed a final 1 mile to the camp.

Another worthwhile tour is found just on the other side of the highway from the campground. Here, you'll find FR 830. Drive north on this road for about 11 miles and you'll find several good vantage points and places to wander or picnic.

Field Notes
I've seen only one camper here in five visits during the summer season. Visitation is higher during the fall hunting season.

Directions
From Devils Tower in Wyoming, take HWY 24 eastward for 27 miles. If traveling from South Dakota, head west from the town of Belle Fourche on HWY 34 (in South Dakota) and HWY 24 (in Wyoming) for 25.5 miles. The campground is on the south side of the highway.

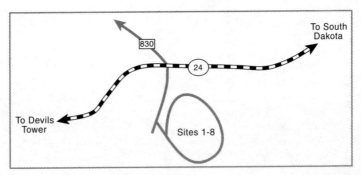

3 Cook Lake Recreation Area
Lakeside camping in Wyoming's Black Hills

Map	Page 146
Usage	Moderate to high
Sites	33
Cost	$15-$17 ($10 in the off season)
Camp Facilities	Fire rings, picnic tables, water, pit toilets, trash containers
Spur Length	Long—up to 45 feet
Managing Agency	USDA Forest Service—Black Hills National Forest; a host is on site
Reservations	Accepted—check www.recreation.gov or call (877) 444-6777
Season	Open all year (snowmobile access in the winter)
Elevation	4,750 feet
GPS Coordinates	N44° 35.4' W104° 24.29'

The Camp
Devils Tower aside, Cook Lake is the premier destination in Wyoming's Black Hills. Centrally located in the Bear Lodge Mountains, the recreation area includes a small lake, picnic area, hiking trails, and two separated camping areas. Compared to the Black Hills in South Dakota, you'll find this recreation site to be a quiet outdoor retreat although it's growing in popularity and weekends see a fair amount of traffic.

Cook Lake

The campground consists of Loop A (sites 1–18) and Loop B (sites 19–33) with the former being closer to the lake's shoreline. Eight sites in Loop A are walk-in tent sites that offer more privacy than the others and are offered at a lower nightly rate. Loop B is perched in a ponderosa pine forest above the lake—nearly 100 feet higher—with a few sites in direct view of the water. You'll find the parking spurs in Loop B to be more inviting to those longer RVs and trailers.

Most campsites receive shade, but there are a few in both loops that are treeless and sit under a bright sky. Except for the busier weekends during the summer, you'll find plenty of vacant sites here, especially in the upper loop, so you'll enjoy plenty of space between campers.

Anglers will find brown and rainbow trout in Cook Lake. Boaters are welcome, but only manually-powered craft or electric motors are permitted. There is a separate parking area for anglers.

A 1-mile trail loops around the lake. A longer option is the 3.5-mile Cliff Swallow Trail. Open to mountain bikes, horses, and hikers, the trail explores a short ridge above the Beaver Creek drainage. Both trails are family friendly.

Field Notes

If you want a quiet camping vacation for your family, stay here during the middle of the week. Weekends bring more traffic and louder campers.

Directions

From Sundance, drive west on HWY 14 for 2 miles. Turn north onto FR 838 and drive 19 miles following the signs for the Cook Lake Recreation Area. The pavement ends after the first 8 miles and the road then turns to gravel. Turn west onto FR 842 and proceed 1 mile to the camp.

To get there from HWY 24 to the north, drive west from Alva for 5 miles and then turn south on FR 838. Bear left at the junction and follow FR 832 south for 8 miles to reach the turnoff.

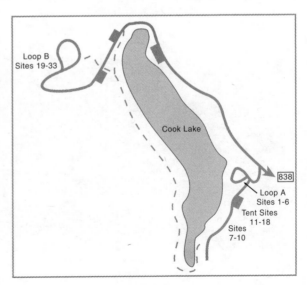

Loop B
Sites 19-33

Cook Lake

838

Loop A
Sites 1-6
Tent Sites
11-18
Sites
7-10

4 Sundance Horse Camp
Wyoming Black Hills' horse camp and trailhead

Map	Page 146
Usage	Low
Sites	10
Cost	$17
Camp Facilities	Fire rings, picnic tables, water, pit toilets, trash containers, corrals, mounting ramp, feed bunks
Spur Length	Long—up to 45 feet
Managing Agency	USDA Forest Service—Black Hills National Forest
Reservations	Accepted—check www.recreation.gov or call (877) 444-6777
Season	Open mid-May until snow closure
Elevation	4,800 feet
GPS Coordinates	N44° 26.56' W104° 20.9'

The Camp

Sundance Horse Camp is on the eastern edge of Wyoming's Bear Lodge Mountains where the pines meet the grassy plains. As a result of straddling the national forest boundary, the camp has no trees, shade, or privacy from other campers. What it does offer is a terrific view over a broad valley where whitetail deer often forage.

Sundance Horse Camp

The ten main campsites are spaced along a couple of gravel lanes. The parking spurs are long, level, and wheelchair accessible. You'll have no problem putting a truck and horse trailer into one of these spots. Camping is also permitted in the main parking area for self-contained horse trailers and tow vehicles.

The camp is well equipped for pack animals and riders. There are six corrals that each hold four horses and two feed bunks that accommodate eight animals each. Hitching posts and a rider mounting ramp, for those with disabilities, also adds to the camp's accessibility features.

The camp's trailhead is an entry point to 54 miles of trails in the Carson Draw and Sundance trail system. These trails make excellent rides, or hikes, and are open to hoof and foot traffic, mountain biking, and cross-country skiing. Most of them gain less than a couple hundred feet in elevation. The Forest Service has a trail brochure that includes maps and route information.

Field Notes
Unlike the horse camps in neighboring South Dakota, you can get away with camping here without horses and you won't be waiting in line for a spot. I've visited this campground several times over the years and have never seen a camper here.

Directions
From Sundance, travel east on HWY 14 for 1 mile. Turn north onto Government Valley Road and drive 2 miles to the camp.

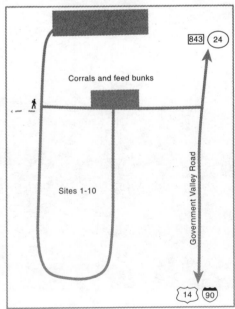

5 Reuter Campground
Mountain camp near I-90

Map	Page 146
Usage	Low
Sites	24
Cost	$12
Camp Facilities	Fire rings, picnic tables, water, pit toilets, trash containers
Spur Length	Medium—up to 30 feet
Managing Agency	USDA Forest Service—Black Hills National Forest; a host is on site
Reservations	Accepted—check www.recreation.gov or call (877) 444-6777
Season	Open late May until snow closure
Elevation	5,450 feet
GPS Coordinates	N44° 25.55' W104° 25.39'

The Camp

Reuter Campground is just a few miles northwest of Sundance, a small, charming Wyoming town that sits on I-90. The camp's close proximity to the Interstate and easy driving on paved roads make this a great spot if you're just passing through to bigger destinations like Yellowstone. It also works well as a base from which you can explore Wyoming's Black Hills and Devils Tower.

Reuter Campground

The campground has two loops that are shaded by a mature forest of ponderosa pine. Parking spurs are spacious and decently spaced. If you have a large trailer or RV, these will be the most accessible sites that you'll find in the Bear Lodge Mountains, though the spurs at Cook Lake Campground are longer.

There are plenty of things to do in this area. The nearest is a trailhead just west of the camp entrance that accesses 54 miles of trails in the Carson Draw, Reuter's Spring, and Sundance trail networks. The trails make for excellent mountain biking and horse rides as well as day hikes for the family. Most of them gain less than a couple hundred feet in elevation. The Forest Service has a trail brochure that includes maps and route information.

For motorized exploration, a drive to the north will take you across this small mountain range. A great overlook is just a few minutes away at Warren Lookout Tower, which is still in use today. Further north yet, you'll find the Cook Lake Recreation Area where there is another campground, picnic area, more trails, and a fishing lake.

Field Notes

Surprisingly, the host is often the only occupant at this campground. If you're looking for a little solitude out of the summer heat, this is the spot.

Directions

From Sundance, head west on HWY 14 for 2 miles and turn north onto FR 838 (watch for the Cook Lake Recreation Area sign). Travel 2.5 miles on the paved road to the campground.

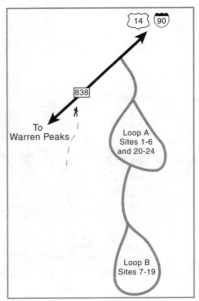

Devils Tower National Monument

Devils Tower is a 1,267-foot igneous rock column—possibly an old volcano core—that pierces the big Wyoming sky. It creates a distinctive landmark that can be seen for miles. Standing alone above a rolling landscape of mixed grass and forest, the eroding tower is impressive, a bit weird, and photogenic from both near and far. The site is held sacred by many American Indians who have a differing account on how the tower was formed. Rock climbers also prize the structure for its challenging routes to the summit. The recreation area features a campground, hiking trails, and visitor center.

6 Belle Fourche Campground
Streamside camp next to Devils Tower

Map	Page 146
Usage	High
Sites	50; 3 group sites
Cost	$12. A daily park entrance fee or annual pass is also required.
Camp Facilities	Grills, picnic tables, water, restrooms, trash containers, dump station
Spur Length	Medium—up to 30 feet
Managing Agency	National Park Service
Reservations	Not accepted—first come, first served
Season	Open early April through October
Elevation	3,855 feet
GPS Coordinates	N44° 34.92' W104° 42.4'

The Camp

This campground sits a little over a half mile from Devils Tower along the grassy banks of the Belle Fourche River (Fourche is pronounced "foosh"). From this bustling spot, you'll have a short drive or hike to the recreation area's other facilities.

The two-loop campground is covered by large cottonwood trees that shade the campsites. Temperatures can soar like the tower itself at this elevation, but the trees (and breeze) help make summer afternoons more comfortable. The parking spurs are mostly level pull-throughs that accommodate RVs as easily as tent campers.

There are three group sites (B9-B12) available at a cost of $2 per person. Each site must be occupied by at least six people with a maximum group size of 20. Four vehicles are allowed at each spot.

There are five trails that explore the Devils Tower area. The Joyner Ridge Trail is a 1.5-mile loop at the north end of the park. Conversely, the South Side-Valley View Trail forms a 1.2-mile hike near the campground to the south. The most popular trails are Tower Trail and Red Beds Trail, which form loops around the tower. The Tower Trail is the shortest route at 1.3-miles and circles the base of the rock structure. Red Beds is longer and forms a 3-mile loop that extends into the northeast corner of the park. All trails are suitable for family hiking.

Devils Tower from Belle Fourche Campground

If you're interested in climbing the tower, which is a technical climb, be sure to contact the park service before planning a trip. There are annual closures to protect nesting prairie falcons, and the park service discourages climbing during June out of respect for American Indians.

Field Notes

This is a very popular tourist attraction and traffic through the campground is high. Fall is an especially beautiful time to visit. Belle Fourche Campground is the only public camp at Devils Tower, but there is also a privately-owned KOA near the monument's entrance.

Directions

From Gillette, drive east on I-90 for 26 miles to Moorcroft. Drive north on HWY 14A for 26 miles to HWY 24. You can also take HWY 14 west from Sundance for 20 miles to this junction. Take HWY 24 north for 6 miles.

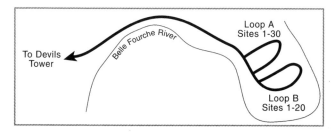

Keyhole State Park

Keyhole State Park is centered around a large reservoir in northeastern Wyoming where the rugged terrain of the Black Hills concedes to open prairie. The park consists of sagebrush flats on the west side and sparse pine forests on the eastern half. Keyhole Reservoir was created in 1952 and holds 14,720 acres of water. Anglers can find northern pike, channel catfish, and walleye. The wetlands also provide habitat for up to 225 species of migrating birds. During the summer, there are osprey, white pelican, common yellowthroat, wild turkeys, and savannah sparrow. Bald eagles can be observed during the winter months.

7 Keyhole State Park Campgrounds
Reservoir camping west of the Black Hills

Map	Page 146, 162
Usage	Moderate
Sites	283
Cost	$10-$17. A daily park entrance fee or annual pass is also required.
Camp Facilities	Fire rings, picnic tables, water, pit toilets, water and electric hookups (Tatanka campground only), trash containers, dump station
Spur Length	Long—up to 60 feet
Managing Agency	Wyoming State Parks
Reservations	Accepted—check www.wyo-park.com or call (877) 996-7275
Season	Open all year
Elevation	4,100 feet
GPS Coordinates	N44° 21.37' W104° 45.3'

The Camps

Keyhole State Park includes eight campgrounds along the eastern bays of the reservoir and another two in the middle of the park near the town of Pine Haven. Facilities vary between the camps, but all of them have fire rings and pit toilets at a minimum.

The most northern camp, Rocky Point, is near the reservoir's dam and includes 16 primitive sites that are mostly in the open. Nearby Cottonwood Campground is larger and offers a pine forest, playground, and covered group picnic shelter.

Other nearby campgrounds—Pronghorn, Homestead, Arch Rock, Beach, Tatanka, and Pat's Point—are mostly open camps though some sites are covered by pines. These are the largest campgrounds in the park and they collectively offer more than 150 sites. Most of these have gravel parking spurs (both back-in sites and pull-throughs) and a few are

Campsites at Keyhole State Park

handicap accessible. If you're looking for easy access to the water, check out Pat's Point which also has a boat ramp that can be used when water levels are high. The handful of undeveloped sites at Beach Campground sit on unlevel ground making it a poor choice for trailers and RVs.

The premier camp in this group is Tatanka. It offers water and electric hookups, four camping cabins, a dozen tent sites, several picnic sites, a covered group picnic shelter, and decent shade at most of the spots. This campground requires reservations during the peak season (mid-May to mid-September).

The interior campgrounds—Coulter Bay and Wind Creek—include a total of 30 undeveloped sites and are close to boat ramps. The eastern one, Coulter Bay, has mostly walk-in sites near rock cliffs and no trees. Wind Creek to the west has trees but does not have any potable water.

A marina on the east side of the reservoir provides supplies, groceries, showers, licenses, boat rentals, and a small number of campsites with electric hookups.

Aside from fishing and camping, there is also a 6.2-mile Volksmarch trail that can be walked between Memorial and Labor Day weekends.

Field Notes
Although summer obviously brings the most visitation, spring and fall are considered excellent times to visit. If you do go during the summer, you might shoot for Independence Day. The town of Pine Haven has a fireworks show on July 4th that can be seen from some of the campgrounds. I'm told the best views are from your boat.

Directions

From Gillette, drive east on I-90 for 38 miles and take Exit 165 for Pine Ridge Road. Turn north and drive 7 miles. You can also exit at Moorcroft (26 miles east of Gillette at Exit 154) and drive north on HWY 14 for 5 miles. Turn east on HWY 113 and drive east for 5 miles to reach the turnoff to the park's interior campgrounds, or 8 miles to reach Pine Ridge Road for the eastern camps.

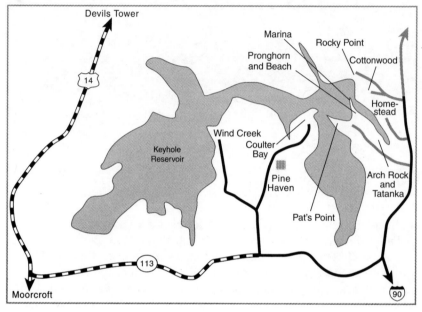

POPULAR ATTRACTIONS
WHERE TO GO, WHAT TO SEE, WHAT TO DO

The Black Hills are filled with attractions ranging from museums and national parks to caverns and tourist traps. This list gives you an overview of some of the most popular sites that you'll read about or encounter along the way.

Angostura Recreation Area
http://gfp.sd.gov/state-parks/directory/angostura

This state park features a huge reservoir that beckons to water lovers and anglers. The site includes four campgrounds, swim beaches, boat ramps, and other facilities.

Badlands National Park
www.nps.gov/badl

This national park has nearly a quarter million acres of mixed-grass prairie and badland formations that shape scenic spires and buttes. The park has a visitor center and two campgrounds. You may spot bison, prairie dogs, bighorn sheep, deer, and pronghorn antelope. The park is accessed from I-90, about an hour east of Rapid City, South Dakota. An entry fee or pass is required.

Bear Butte State Park
http://gfp.sd.gov/state-parks/directory/bear-butte

This state park northeast of I-90 and Sturgis includes camping, trails, a small fishing lake, a visitor center, and a nearly 1,000-foot mountain that sits atop the surrounding plains.

Bear Country USA
www.bearcountryusa.com

This drive-through wildlife park is a privately-owned operation where you get up-close views of bears, wolves, and other wild critters. The park is south of Rapid City, South Dakota on HWY 16. An entry fee is required.

Black Elk Wilderness
http://wilderness.net

The Black Elk Wilderness includes 13,605 acres of land within the Black Hills National Forest that is set aside to retain its primitive and undeveloped character. These lands can only be accessed by foot, hoof, or by wheelchairs, when used as intended. Bicycles and motorized and mechanical equipment of any kind is prohibited. The wilderness includes some of the finest terrain in the Black Hills, including the Harney Range. There are numerous trails that traverse the wilderness. A camping permit is required if backpacking within the wilderness boundary.

Black Hills National Forest
www.fs.usda.gov/bhnf

The Black Hills National Forest encompasses over a million acres of public land in western South Dakota and northeastern Wyoming. You'll find dozens of campgrounds, hundreds of miles of hiking trails and backroads, reservoirs, canyons, and wildlife. The supervisor's office is located north of Custer, South Dakota on HWY 16. Other offices in South Dakota are located in Spearfish, Rapid City, and at Pactola Reservoir. Offices in Wyoming are in Sundance and Newcastle.

Black Hills Wild Horse Sanctuary
www.gwtc.net/~iram

At this sanctuary, you can see hundreds of wild horses as they roam their natural habitat. You can take guided tours of the sanctuary and also find Native American ceremonial sites, petroglyphs, historical buildings, and a gift shop. The sanctuary is found south of Hot Springs, South Dakota on HWY 71. Tour reservations are recommended. Various fees are required, depending on the activity.

Centennial Trail
www.fs.usda.gov/bhnf

This diverse 111-mile route utilizes an old railroad bed that runs from Bear Butte State Park near Sturgis to Wind Cave National Park near Hot Springs, South Dakota. There are 36 trailheads that provide access to horseback riders, hikers, and mountain bikers. Motorized use is allowed on a short portion of the trail in the Black Hills National Forest.

Crazy Horse Memorial
www.crazyhorsememorial.org

Billed as the world's largest mountain carving, this sculpture of a Native American Lakota leader is a work in progress. The site is managed by the Crazy Horse Memorial Foundation, a non-profit organization, and includes the carving, a gift shop, museum, and restaurant. The memorial is located north of Custer, South Dakota on HWY 16/HWY 385. An entry fee is required.

Custer State Park
http://gfp.sd.gov/state-parks/directory/custer

This 71,000-acre state park is located on the southeast side of South Dakota's Black Hills. Encompassing towering rocks, forests, and rolling grasslands, the park's beautiful scenery doubles as critical wildlife habitat for bison, antelope, deer, elk, and other animals. The park offers scenic driving, campgrounds, resorts, lakes, visitor centers, hiking trails, and special programs. An entry fee or pass is required.

Devils Tower
www.nps.gov/deto

This eroding rock structure rises 1,267 feet, creating a fascinating landmark that can be seen for miles. The site includes a campground, visitor center, hiking trails, and special events and programs. The tower is located northeast of Gillette, Wyoming on HWY 24. An entry fee or pass is required.

Ellsworth Air Force Base
www.ellsworth.af.mil

This base is home to the B-1 bomber, which can sometimes be seen flying over the Rapid City and Mount Rushmore area. During the summer, a guided bus tour of the base starts from the South Dakota Air and Space Museum. To reach the museum from I-90, take Exit 69 just minutes east of Rapid City.

Evan's Plunge
www.evansplunge.com

Claiming to be the world's largest natural warm-water indoor pool, this center offers waterslides, hot tubs, and lots of fun for the kids. It's located off HWY 385 on the north side of Hot Springs, South Dakota.

Flintstones Bedrock City
www.flintstonesbedrockcity.com

This private theme park and campground is based on the popular stone-age cartoon. You can tour Bedrock City, take a train ride, ride in the Flintmobile, play mini-golf or arcade games, or eat at the drive-in restaurant. The park is easily spotted in the town of Custer.

George S. Mickelson Trail

http://gfp.sd.gov/state-parks/directory/mickelson-trail

This 109-mile trail runs mostly through the Black Hills National Forest between Deadwood and Edgemont, South Dakota. This former Burlington Northern railroad bed has a gravel surface, low grades (under 4%), more than 100 bridges, four rock tunnels, and 15 trailheads. It's open to foot, hoof, and bicycle traffic.

Gordon Stockade

http://gfp.sd.gov/state-parks/directory/custer

This fort is a reconstructed replica of the one used by Lt. George Custer in the late 1870s when his expedition discovered gold in the Black Hills. The stockade is located on the original site, just east of Custer on HWY 16A near the Custer State Park entrance. Interpretive signs at the stockade explain more of the expedition's history.

Harney Peak

At 7,242 feet, this scenic peak is the highest point in South Dakota as well as east of the Rocky Mountains. A 3.5-mile hike from Sylvan Lake in Custer State Park will gain you the summit where you'll find a lookout tower.

Iron Mountain Road

http://gfp.sd.gov/state-parks/directory/custer

This 17-mile drive follows HWY 16A from Custer State Park to the Mount Rushmore National Memorial. The road is best known for its spiraling pigtail-shaped bridges and rock tunnels that frame Mount Rushmore. Minimum clearances for the tunnels measure 12' wide by 9' 7" high.

Jewel Cave National Monument

www.nps.gov/jeca

This site features the second longest cave in the world, a passage that is at least 153 miles long. A visitor center, hiking trails, and cave tours are available. The park is west of Custer, South Dakota on HWY 16.

Mammoth Site

www.mammothsite.com

As the world's largest mammoth research facility, this center allows you to tour various museum exhibits and an active dig site. The facility is located in Hot Springs, South Dakota along the HWY 18 Bypass. An entry fee is required.

Minuteman Missile National Historic Site

www.nps.gov/mimi

At this historic site, you can tour the facilities used to house and operate the Cold War's Minuteman Missiles, ballistic weapons with nuclear warheads that could travel to the other side of the globe. Tours take you through the personnel's living quarters, the launch control center, and a missile silo. To reach the site from I-90, take Exit 131 about an hour east of Rapid City.

Mount Coolidge Fire Tower

http://gfp.sd.gov/state-parks/directory/custer

This fire lookout tower at 6,023 feet has an observation deck where you can overlook Custer State Park, Mount Rushmore, the Needles, and other regional landmarks. A narrow gravel road leads to the tower and is not suitable for large vehicles, trailers, or RVs. The tower is open to the public from Memorial Day through September. Mount Coolidge is located on HWY 87, just 3 miles south of HWY 16A.

Mount Rushmore National Memorial

www.nps.gov/moru

A renowned mountain sculpture that features the faces of four American presidents: George Washington, Thomas Jefferson, Theodore Roosevelt, and Abraham Lincoln. The site includes a viewing platform, trails, museum, gift shops, an evening lighting ceremony, and various programs and events. The carving is located southwest of Keystone, South Dakota on HWY 244.

Needles Highway

http://gfp.sd.gov/state-parks/directory/custer

The Needles Highway (HWY 87) connects HWY 16/HWY 385 south of Hill City to HWY 16A in Custer State Park. Spanning 14 miles, the road twists and bores through the Harney Range, which includes towering rock spires known as the Needles. The road has tight switchbacks and three narrow tunnels with minimum clearances that measure 9' wide and 10' 4" high.

Norbeck Wildlife Preserve

www.fs.usda.gov/bhnf

This 34,255 acre preserve was established in 1920 to support the area's game animals and birds. It's located north of Custer State Park in the Black Hills National Forest. The center of the preserve includes the Black Elk

Wilderness. These primitive lands include many miles of backcountry trails for horseback riders and hikers.

Peter Norbeck Scenic Byway
http://peternorbeck.americasbyways.net

This byway creates a 70-mile loop through the southern Black Hills by incorporating Iron Mountain Road (HWY 16A) south of Keystone, HWY 244 between Keystone and Hill City, and the Needles Highway (HWY 87) northeast of Custer. The Needles Highway and Iron Mountain Road both have tight switchbacks and narrow tunnels.

Reptile Gardens
www.reptilegardens.com

This is a privately-owned wildlife park that features gardens and a variety of exotic birds, reptiles, amphibians, and bugs. The exhibit is located on HWY 16 south of Rapid City, South Dakota. An entry fee is required.

Roughlock Falls Nature Area
http://gfp.sd.gov/state-parks/directory/roughlock-falls

These cascades are a popular attraction in Spearfish Canyon. A walkway with overlooks and interpretive signs is provided next to the scenic drainage. The falls are located off of HWY 14A between Spearfish and Cheyenne Crossing on FR 222.

South Dakota Air and Space Museum
www.sdairandspacemuseum.com

This museum features over two dozen military aircraft and missile displays. During the summer, you can also take a guided bus tour of nearby Ellsworth Air Force Base. To reach the museum from I-90, take Exit 69 just minutes east of Rapid City. Admission is free.

Spearfish Canyon
www.fs.usda.gov/bhnf

This remarkable canyon is composed of limestone cliffs, steep timbered hillsides, and waterfalls. Spearfish Creek flows through the canyon and is paralleled by the Spearfish Canyon Scenic Byway (HWY 14A). This scenic roadway runs for about 20 miles between Spearfish and Cheyenne Crossing.

Sturgis Motorcycle Rally

www.sturgismotorcyclerally.com

Held annually in early August, this massive gathering brings hundreds of thousands of bikers to Sturgis, South Dakota and the greater region. The rally includes vendors, events, and, of course, mind-boggling numbers of motorcycles.

Wall Drug

www.walldrug.com

This sprawling one-of-a-kind store has it all. Among the many departments, you'll find food, pharmacy, souvenirs, gifts, toys, books, jewelry, clothes, boots, arcade, chapel, picnic area, and even an animated T-Rex. You'll run out of time before you run out of things to see. The store is located in Wall, South Dakota on I-90 east of Rapid City near Badlands National Park.

Wildlife Loop Road

http://gfp.sd.gov/state-parks/directory/custer

This paved 18-mile road loops through the southern portion of Custer State Park. The route features rolling grasslands that are filled with wildlife such as bison and antelope. You may also spot coyotes, elk, and even a few begging burros. The eastern terminus is on HWY 16A on the east side of the park. The western terminus is on HWY 87 near the Blue Bell Lodge.

Wind Cave National Park

www.nps.gov/wica

This park features one of the world's longest and most complex cave systems. Above ground, the park's grasslands and forests serve as critical habitat to the area's wildlife. The park includes a visitor center, campground, hiking trails, and a variety of underground cave tours. The site is located north of Hot Springs, South Dakota on HWY 385.

CONTACTS
FOR MORE INFORMATION

When planning a trip, it's a good idea to contact the managing agency of the area where you'll be visiting. The agency can update you about special events, closures, construction, weather, and other things you might want to know before leaving home.

USDA Forest Service - Black Hills National Forest
www.fs.usda.gov/bhnf

Forest Supervisor's Office
1019 N. 5th Street
Custer, SD 57730
Phone: (605) 673-9200

Mystic Ranger District
8221 South Hwy 16
Rapid City, SD 57702
Phone: (605) 343-1567

Northern Hills Ranger District
2014 N. Main Street
Spearfish, SD 57783
Phone: (605) 642-4622

Pactola Visitor Center
(Located on HWY 385 at
Pactola Reservoir)
Phone: (605) 343-8755

Hell Canyon Ranger District
330 Mt. Rushmore Road
Custer, SD 57730
Phone: (605) 673-4853

Bearlodge Ranger District
101 S. 21st Street
P.O. Box 680
Sundance, WY 82729
Phone: (307) 283-1361

Hell Canyon Ranger District
1225 Washington Street
Newcastle, WY 82729
Phone: (307) 746-2782

National Park Service (national parks, monuments, and memorials)
www.nps.gov

Badlands National Park
www.nps.gov/badl
25216 Ben Reifel Road/P.O. Box 6
Interior, SD 57750
Phone: (605) 433-5361

Devils Tower National Monument
www.nps.gov/deto
P.O. Box 10
Devils Tower, WY 82714-0010
Phone: (307) 467-5283

Jewel Cave National Monument
www.nps.gov/jeca
11149 US Highway 16
Building B12
Custer, SD 57730
Phone: (605) 673-8300

Wind Cave National Park
www.nps.gov/wica
26611 US Highway 385
Hot Springs, SD 57747-6027
Phone: (605) 745-4600

South Dakota Game , Fish and Parks

http://gfp.sd.gov/state-parks

20641 SD Highway 1806
Fort Pierre, SD 57532
Phone: (605) 223.7660

U.S. Army Corps of Engineers

http://corpslakes.usace.army.mil/visitors

Box 664
Chamberlain, SD 57325-9801
Phone: (605) 745-5476

Wyoming Game and Fish

http://gf.state.wy.us

5400 Bishop Boulevard
Cheyenne, WY 82006
Phone: (307) 777-4600

Wyoming State Parks, Historic Sites & Trails

http://wyoparks.state.wy.us

Barrrett Building - 4th Floor
2301 Central Avenue
Cheyenne, WY 82002
Phone: (307) 777-6323

Index

L

Legion Lake Campground, 114

M

Minuteman Missile National
  Historic Site, 168
Moon Campground, 71
Mount Coolidge Fire Tower, 168
Mount Rushmore National
  Memorial, 168

N

Needles Highway, 168
Norbeck Wildlife Preserve, 168

O

Oreville Campground, 91

P

Pactola Campground, 52
Pactola Reservoir, 51
Pat's Point Campground, 160
Peter Norbeck Scenic Byway, 169
Pronghorn Campground, 160

R

Redbank Springs Campground, 69
Reuter Campground, 155
Rocky Point Campground, 160
Rocky Point Recreation Area, 30
Rod and Gun Campground, 37
Roubaix Lake Campground, 47
Roughlock Falls Nature Area, 169

S

Sage Creek Campground, 140
Sand Creek Public Access Area, 147
Shady Rest Non-Profit Youth
  Camp, 116
Sheridan Lake Southside
  Campground, 75
Sheridan North Cove Group
  Campground, 73

South Dakota Air and Space
  Museum, 169
Spearfish Canyon, 169
Spearfish City Campground, 35
Stockade Lake Group Camp, 112
Stockade Lake North
  Campground, 108
Stockade Lake South
  Campground, 110
Sundance Horse Camp, 153
Sylvan Lake Campground, 101

T

Tatanka Campground, 160
Timon Campground, 39

W

Whitetail Campground, 63
Wildlife Loop Road, 170
Willow Creek Horse Camp, 82
Wind Cave National Park, 129
Wind Creek Campground, 161
Wrinkled Rock Climber's
  Trailhead Camp, 84

About the Author

When Marc Smith isn't sitting behind a desk as a technical writer for the USDA Forest Service, he likes to explore the backcountry of the Rocky Mountain West with his family. In addition to the book you are holding, Marc has written three other guidebooks: Hiking Wyoming's Medicine Bow National Forest, The Wyoming Camping Guide, and Wyoming Backroads. He also stays busy by serving on a search and rescue team.

  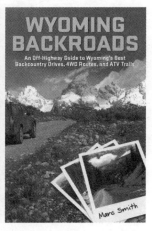

Open Space Publications

Updates to this guide can be found at www.OpenSpacePublications.com. If you have a question, need another book, or just want to share your trip notes, you can contact us by letter, phone, or email.

Open Space Publications, LLC
PO Box 50133
Casper, WY 82605-0133

Website: www.OpenSpacePublications.com
Phone: (888) 677-6423
Email: info@openspacepublications.com